BOOK COLLECTING
AS ONE OF THE FINE ARTS

BOOK COLLECTING
AS ONE OF THE
FINE ARTS

and Other Essays

COLIN FRANKLIN

SCOLAR PRESS

Published by
SCOLAR PRESS   Ashgate Publishing Company
Gower House   Old Post Road
Croft Road   Brookfield
Aldershot   Vermont 05036-9704
Hants GU11 3HR   USA
England

British Library Cataloguing-in-Publication Data.

Franklin, Colin
  Book Collecting as One of the Fine Arts
  and Other Essays
  I.   Title
  824.914

Library of Congress Cataloging-in-Publication Data.

Franklin, Colin.
  Book collecting as one of the fine arts, and other essays / Colin Franklin.

  Contents: Book collecting as one of the fine arts—Type under the water—Garlands of Rachel—Print and design in eighteenth-century editions of Shakespeare—John Baptist Jackson and chiaroscuro—Lord Chesterfield and his Characters—William Combe—A Victorian dining club—D. G. Rossetti—Elizabeth Browning at the mercy of her publishers—Pied Piper—Hume—Sludge & I.

  1. Printing—Great Britain—History—18th century.
2. Printing—Great Britain—History—19th century.   3. Printing—Great Britain—History—20th century.   4. English literature—19th century—History and criticism.   5. Book collecting—Great Britain.
I. Title
Z151.4.F72   1996   95-36426
002-dc20   CIP

ISBN 1 85928 262 8

Typeset in Plantin by Poole Typesetting (Wessex) Ltd and printed in Great Britain by Hartnolls Limited, Bodmin

Contents

To Alan and Miranda

Preface

It is a bookseller's privilege to stray from subject to subject, and we don't always like to be type-cast. Thus I have become acquainted with private presses, mezzotint prints, aquatint illustrations, early colour-printing, and Japan. If a fence divides the visual from the textual, my interest has been – by mere idleness perhaps – more with the former.

But not entirely, as I hope these essays show. Eighteenth-century Shakespeare is a wonderful subject, because editors anxious to reveal and clarify every phrase of the plays quarrelled so passionately in their footnotes. Chesterfield arrived through the presence of a large assembly of partly unpublished manuscript. The short Rossetti piece excited me as a minor discovery many years ago, when I was involved as a publisher with authors who had seen ghosts or produced automatic writing. The last three essays, on the Brownings, are the result of several periods spent at the Armstrong Browning Library, Baylor University, Texas.

'Garlands of Rachel' and the Shakespeare essay appeared in the *Book Collector*; 'Lord Chesterfield and his *Characters*' is adapted from a talk to the Friends of the Bodleian, the Rossetti piece from *Essays In Criticism*; the first essay was prepared for a congress in Cleveland, Ohio, and 'Ye Sette of Odd Volumes' was written for the Club of Odd Volumes in Boston; 'John Baptist Jackson' was read to the Printing Historical Society. Most are printed here for the first time; I am grateful for permission to reprint those which are not, and to Scolar Press for their sympathetic approach to this book.

In an overflow of gratitude for nearly half a century among books, I should mention especially three other institutions in the United States where I have received much kindness through months or semesters of particular focus: Bridwell Library, Southern Methodist

University, Dallas, Texas; the University of Tulsa, Oklahoma; and the Lilly Library, University of Indiana, at Bloomington, where unpublished Browning manuscripts, from which I have quoted freely, now rest.

1

Book Collecting as One of the Fine Arts

The rather precious title of this essay is taken from Lord David Cecil, whose inaugural lecture as Goldsmith's professor of English, at Oxford in 1949, was called *Reading as One of the Fine Arts*. 'I am always biased in favour of anything expensive and ornamental and useless', Cecil told his Oxford audience, and said 'the primary object of a student of literature is to be delighted. His duty is to enjoy himself; his efforts should be directed to developing his faculty of appreciation. For this reason' he added, 'I thought it might be worth while giving up this afternoon to considering what the development of such a faculty entails'.

Expensive, ornamental, useless. If the first is troublesome, the second may often be true of books and the third strikes a special chord. 'What do you specialise in?' I am so often asked as a bookseller, and the only honest embracing reply would be 'Useless books'.

We can face with ease the worry of expense, as the least subtle of any, for either we have money or haven't, and my assumption now, whether appropriate or offensive, is that we haven't. There are indeed problems in taste for the rich, as for the rest of us, because at any level collecting means rejecting.

One great difference, still in the theme of money and cost, is that many people might have managed it then; they needed no colossal supply of wealth to form a wonderful collection across the spectrum of early manuscript and printed books, thirty or forty years ago. The near-impossibility of achieving that now, a stimulant perhaps to the few, has changed the character of book-collecting because prices, as with other forms of art, have begun to lose touch with what they buy.

1

Not another word now about money; the dilemma of those who desire but cannot afford is more interesting.

Paradox gives us who collect books, privately or for libraries or sale, a special position among all such artists; we are the privileged, and may easily agree these odd artefacts have lost their function in a way that pictures, for instance, have not. The National Gallery in London has opened its beautiful Sainsbury wing where visitors view early church art from Italy, looted or bought in years gone by, desecrated, in marvellous condition, superbly shown. Of course we should kneel and pray before them: they should never have left the altars and shrines. Instead we admire, read captions perhaps, hope to remember a name and its date, congratulate ourselves upon a new sprinkle of culture; yet we see them as paintings, subjects not merely objects, a little of their purpose crosses the vast divide. And our eyes, crossing their surface, cause no damage.

Books are more complex – presences, alive or dead. We see their backs, or the backs of their boxes. At the home of a collector in New York I admired rows of binders' boxes, blue and red morocco on his shelves, and asked if I might look inside a few. 'Ah no' he said, 'you see those are just boxes, the books are in the bank'. I suppose they were presences in his mind, and book-collecting is a private affair. I do not report the episode with any overtone of criticism. He took them out from time to time, physically or mentally.

The surprise when we look at more than the spine of a book is better than the diminishing response provided by any painting we see every day on the wall. In this lucky intermediate period which happens to be ours, we may hope to own quite a large number of books, and none is likely to be opened very often. Apart from our surprise each time, illustrations and illuminations live in the dark, never fading. Poor paper may decay but the colours do not. They keep their secret.

Most people have no idea how to handle a book. There lingers in many institutions an appalling concept of the 'working copy', of precious books as quarry for scholarship. If our minds are tuned to the fine art of book-collecting, scholarship touches it only at a tangent. We may learn by choosing of course, and by owning, but that brings less than scholarship. For those who must tease the meaning from text – microfilm and copier, reprint and paperback are wonderful inventions to the rescue of many delicate volumes which such investigators need never hold.

Samuel Johnson, who could not afford to collect, thought Garrick should have sent and lent his exceedingly rare Shakespeare quartos, material of that sort, for his use in preparing an edition of the plays.

Garrick in those generous days was ready and willing for Johnson to use them, but only in his own library, and that struck the great man as an insult. 'But, indeed', Boswell says, 'considering the slovenly and careless manner in which the books were treated by Johnson, it could not be expected that scarce and valuable editions should have been lent to him'.

As paradox afflicts and affects the book collector, I believe librarians responsible for special collections such as exist abundantly in the United States are never free of it. I know they are lovers of books who take delight in acquiring them, yet they face a terrible dilemma in presenting their case for buying, adding to the collections; for most institutions reasonably insist upon some justification in academic need – and the truth is, almost every time, that there is none. Should all that money be spent instead on another student hostel, or swimming pool – or, if earmarked for library use, on the current fetish, conservation? Should not the whole place be deacidified, before another book gets bought?

The problem is sometimes a philosophical one, of what to do with perfect opportunities. A blameless, duty-less day dawns – how to use it? Great pages of finest paper are there, how shall they be filled? All conditions exist for the expansion of collections, and what is done more often than not? Retreat into the safety of conservation, or pull down the library and build an expensive new one, only to face again the fear of what to do with it.

What is the use of a dead book? I was shown at Wordsworth's cottage a copy of De Quincey's *Opium Eater* in boards, perfectly surviving across two centuries. 'What should we do with this?' Robert Woof asked. 'We aren't book collectors, but I don't feel scholars should really open this and use it. What should one do?' Well, the negative answer is that scholars should not get near it – and there could be no reason why they should. A more positive reply would be to suggest a division which must be seen to exist, between the working library and a book museum. I am supposing that all three forms of book collector – private, institutional or commercial – have their hearts in the right place, which is of course the book museum. There, as in any courteous museum, in proper circumstances one may be allowed carefully to touch, hold, turn the leaves.

Collections and museums, whatever their subjects, may have a specialised or more general character. All collections, collectors, whims and tastes should be viewed with sympathetic understanding; yet I am fascinated by the fine barrier which divides connoisseurship from neurosis. In a general, genial way all collectors are neurotic, obsessional, perfectionist. Opening at random a catalogue which arrived in this morning's post, a proper bibliographic description of one of Pope's poetic Epistles, 1738, calls it 'the second issue, with "fools" altered to "Tools" in the last line of p.10'. It does make me wonder whether collectors have been altered from Tools to Fools of this subject, servants of the second issue: of such footling points is our happiness commonly built, mystic excitement confounded by psychotic detail.

Of course one understands it, the whole area of detail: first-issue points, blank leaves present, dust jackets as the day they were born, all of us together in the madhouse of obsession. 'I just had to get it', said an excited friend, 'it was a millimetre taller than the Pforzheimer copy'. I remember John Sparrow's definition of the book collector as having two pleasures, of which the first was to remark 'Now I have the complete set', and the second 'but I don't think you do, do you?'.

For twenty-five years I have lived and eaten from buying and selling books, but question whether it was time honourably spent. For two decades before that, lazy in a family publishing firm, Routledge and Kegan Paul, I was at least helping authors to appear in print. Raising the price of old books is not of service to the world. The temptation to withdraw totally from it all, retire to a cottage and work for prisoners, exists. That should in honesty be declared, but in a less anarchic way there are constructive changes, new ways, which strike me as possible in the altered world of books; for it has greatly changed, and for the worse. Insofar as they are for the rich we may dismiss rich books, like grotesquely priced art, as forms of display – though they used not to be, just three decades ago.

From this confusion it is possible for book-collecting to rise, I believe, as one of the fine arts; but the change of habit will be hard, as are all good resolves in old age, and for a start we could try to distinguish rarity from merit, and perfection from interest.

Recently in Ireland I rescued from a crowded shop floor two large boxes of almost valueless, totally absorbing books. The provenance was apt, a Catholic Mission library; for these many large quartos from the seventeenth century, printed at the Propaganda Fide in Rome, were the heart of the Counter-Reformation, educating Jesuits to carry their mission to far countries. These great books, some of them incomplete, uncut in their old blue paper covers, went into my car and out through a plague of midges to the small bedroom in Connemara where I tried to make sense of each. They stretch across my long table now, more powerful presences than would be a shelf filled with large-paper copies and immaculate Ashendenes.

Leaf-books we know about, leaves we like. Persian miniatures more often that not are leaves from books (I was amazed years ago to discover in Japan the wonder of comparable art in available books), and printers sometimes like to decorate their walls with typographic examples. Visiting the Book of Kells in Dublin of course we view, as at any exhibition, one double-page opening. Chapter-heads, title pages, unpressed leaves with their natural margins – should not a few of these from any one work satisfy us adequately? It is to make a virtue of necessity. 'Find new subjects if the old are too extravagant', we are often told; yet I prefer to suppose the whole book world is still open for those who choose to enjoy it.

Is this an invitation to booksellers to break books? It is not, because well-to-do perfectionists will continue to pay more for complete objects – indeed, I am not expecting these words to have the smallest influence on the conduct or habits of anyone; but I wish to advocate imperfection. Thus gates to delight might be unlocked, we could all scatter among the immense possibilities of books to experience them by choosing, holding and owning.

It is the privilege of a bookseller to wander across subjects, and sometimes to wonder about specialists. Book-collecting runs parallel with reading, in a different medium. In his later years T. E. Lawrence thought only Shakespeare worth reading. A Texan bibliophile limits his collection to Dutch editions of *The Pilgrim's Progress*. Yet it is important in this strange art to feel the power to stray where we choose.

Since focusing long ago on William Morris and his followers I have strayed erratically without much art, and can no more discover a guiding principle now than when I desired two little calf-bound volumes of Robinson Crusoe in the shop-window I passed on my way to school and home. Beyond range of pocket money as they were, my mother gave me the shilling which bought them. I never read Robinson Crusoe until about ten years ago when Gordan Craig's copy, and the woodblocks he engraved to illustrate an edition of it, came into my possession. The experience gave no great pleasure. I do not think my mother's shilling was wasted, for a collector's art is linked with desire which may be quite severed from the function of reading; or if, for example, he collects glass, from the function of drinking.

Perhaps one delight in any sort of collecting is its folly, a separation from practical affairs; in that sense, the heart and spirit of holiday. A clock-collector has no need to check the time so very frequently, nobody *needs* pictures. Japanese swords are not now used, the first edition of Homer in Greek will not be read, I dare say, with poetic pleasure by its owner.

If books offer mysticism close to religion, and choice represents a moment of identity, any criticism for reasons of taste would itself be tasteless. I believe in those moments of identity as revelations of a collector's truth, which ought to be embraced and obeyed. They are easily recognised, as any religious experience, needing no salesman's prompting. The practical brain rebels against a lack of logic, but reasons appear later threading these beads together. Without scheme or shrewdness, a subject is born.

I used to think a great fence divided textual from visual books, a convenient separation, and that my own choice lay with the visual. A dilemma late in life, now, is that *all* books strike me as visual and most have ghosts.

'Did you find any bargains?' is a common, innocent question for which any answer will serve. Every book is a great bargain, if we wanted and own it. If by bargain was meant 'something sold for much less than it is worth', we arrive in deeper waters. It is well to remember, when a bookseller or auctioneer sells the book too cheaply, the other end of the story: whoever owned it before has been deceived. I would say that in the ordinary way of riffling through shelves of a second-hand shop, bargains are not to be found. They were always a coarse concept. Of course if I were to find some book I desired, and it was underpriced, I would buy it – as also, perhaps, if it were overpriced. Desire is the measure of folly. Fellows of Oxford colleges cannot now afford to collect books. When they could, in days that were, their culture triumphed over the un-educated bookseller.

One sound rule exists – follow the spirit. When I first bought books the advice given was excellent: 'Always buy one good thing, rather than several of less importance' – but I would not accept that now, though it may be a shrewd, safe way to behave. So another rule might be, recognise a distinction between taste and safety, what we really want and – the wretched phrase has to be used – safe invest-ment. The two may not be at all the same. I should be far more prosperous now, had I followed safe investment. 'Have you got any history of science?' people used to ask at book fairs, 'any travel, medicine, atlases?' No, I had to tell them, none – perversely, delib-erately, for that is what everyone wanted.

Half the fun - or the art, in my title phrase - is in discovering one's subject, and seeking it. If we must follow the trodden paths, choices are few: have two or three wonderful books, as there may be just several paintings on the walls of a house: that is valid, we may come to that, a private library at such levels belongs to other centuries; or accept leaves and imperfect copies. Both are rational, proper pos-sibilities, yet I am reminded of a favourite line in *Henry IV*, when the Prince says ironically to Poins 'Never a man's thought in the world keeps the roadway better than thine'. I recognise that anyone likes to feel he is laying out his money sensibly, and by choosing landmark-books he will not be ruining his family.

That may also be true in the neurotic world of issue-points, and the even crazier realm, as I view it, of dust jackets. Turning at random again to that catalogue which was quoted earlier, here is 'The first issue of the first edition, with the words "ONE SHILLING" in upper case'. There is *some* sense in it, for the mind which needs total reassurance; its first issue was how that work hit the world. If the shilling were downgraded later in the print run, to lower case, I cannot feel the change was anything to write home about, or hang a price upon, or prove. And such proofs are built upon shifting sand. We live in fear of the next post-graduate researcher from Cambridge, Tokyo or Wyoming, whose article in the Journal of Bibliographical Absurdities will demonstrate that the lower-case shilling was issued first. What will we do then, but say like Macbeth when he learns that Fleance, the son of Banquo, still lives, 'then comes my fit again'?

Title pages offer questionable evidence of the same sort. It is normal practice for publishers to print more sheets of a book than will at first be used, binding the rest by hundreds or five-hundreds as needed. That seems to have been true of the seventeenth century also, when *Paradise Lost* was printed, but the publisher in 1667 and 1668 ordered slightly differing title pages also as the sheets were ordered for binding; and oh! the fuss about those title pages. Should not the first printing of *Paradise Lost*, like the daily round and common task, furnish all we ought to ask? Who cares when the publisher ordered a new supply of existing sheets? Booksellers and bibliographers make a very large matter of it, prices soar – but beware the shifting sands! Learned articles demonstrate that 1668 really preceded 1667, by what logic I have not troubled to understand. Dismay, I suppose, among owners of the 1667, quite unexpected elation for all the class of '68. It would be understandable within the radius of enthusiasm if booksellers, honestly presenting the evidence, were tempted to slant it towards what they happen to own.

Calculate and invest, of course, if calculation and investment excite you. As to dust jackets, I can only declare with conviction that they are the lunacy of the moment; but as all aspects of collecting are replete with lunacy, no critical weight should be felt from that. If you follow the only golden rule I know – listen to the book, not to the bibliographers – it may be that modern authors in blameless dust jackets sound like Mozart in your ears. It is all moderately understandable: that is how those books appeared, how they were first seen by the world, not in naked pseudo-cloth but dressed thus. Yet I am astounded that institutions and collectors spend their resources on dust jackets.

My own pleasures have been on the whole among books printed on hand-made paper; and to limit the seeming vacuity of that, remember it includes any volume printed before about 1820, as well as the smaller theme of what is called 'modern fine printing'. Even ugly, early Shakespeare was printed on hand-made paper, for there were no machines and the evils of wrong chemistry had not begun. Another vital point about those early books, not always emphasised I think, is that every illustration which appeared in them was an original print: woodcut, engraving, etching, mezzotint, aquatint, lithograph. One and all were 'artist books'; no process-engraving then, electro- or photo-offset. Photography immensely reduced the excitement of books; the marvellous accuracy of modern colour-plates in art books gives only a small echo of the excellence of mezzotint in the eighteenth century, engraving and etching in the seventeenth, whereby those same artists were interpreted. Which would we rather have, a glossy art book about Dutch paintings, or the miraculous colour-prints of Ploos Van Amstel reproducing them? Which do we choose, artists or cameras?

There may be practical accuracies to consider. If my appendix had to be removed, and a book-collecting surgeon suggested that in performing the operation he proposed to use as guide the beautiful atomic mezzotints of Gautier D'Agoty, printed from four colour plates in 1744, I might refer him to the X-ray machine and express a preference for modern method.

Perhaps this has been the confession of a partial hypocrite. As collector when I could afford it, and as bookseller, I have desired marvellous copies and enjoyed the vast privilege of owing them. Upon that philosophy we have lived and eaten in peace. I am not about to make a U-turn now, exchanging such standards for barrows of fifth-rate wrecks. Some defence of professional life exists, against a little living worm of conscience. Now and then it wriggles up, eats through, telling me this is all nonsense. Stop fussing about whether the word SHILLING is in caps, it says; never mind if Fools was altered to Tools on p. 10; and down it goes again below the surface.

Like any fine art, book-collecting ends in mystery. We return to Lord David Cecil's pleasure in that which is ornamental, expensive and useless. My grandfather owned what seemed to me sixty years ago a splendid library, though it was not. With apparent attention I listened as we walked through his woods and fields and he explained – perhaps slightly out of touch with an eleven-year-old – how the

Bible was true, and archaeologists were finding deep down the mud of Noah's flood. I may be reporting inaccurately – but I never really listened. After the walk, as reward for my wretched deceptive behaviour, we would mount slowly to the library and he would give me a book. I do not recall what he gave, certainly I never read them. One at the height of my eyes I greatly desired, a wide blue quarto called *History of the Fan*; of course nothing so grand came my way and I would never have dared ask. I believe it was burnt with most of his books, after his death, by a bomb in the war.

No less important than the books, he taught me how to cut brown paper as covers and flaps tailor-made to protect them before handling or using. He was right and I do it still: don't believe that nonsense about the hand's sweat being good for bindings, it soils them. We would ascend then to his muniment room and put his papers in order, which meant taking down piles of journals from shelves, undoing the string, doing it up again and putting them back. There is nothing in this world so relaxing, I spend mornings and evenings of peace re-arranging my books. This essay is written in memory of those boring walks, his library, the muniment room and such books as I received.

2

Type Under the Water

Part of the arts-and-crafts concept of a book, which grew at the end of last century in the Revival of Printing, was that its maker should view the whole as a single work of art – paper, printing, type – and not as a job to be designed and then farmed out to the artificers. William Morris and Emery Walker were pioneers of this, but others followed, developing and rebelling or imitating, so that now we can look back upon this period of the private presses as an important and strange phase in the history of books.

Ricketts, whose Vale Press was one of the finest, clearly defined this ideal:

> A Kelmscott book, and, if I may say so, a Vale book, is a living and corporate whole, the quality of beauty therein is all-pervading; it is not decorated as a modern house is decorated by the upholsterer and the picture dealer, it is conceived harmoniously and made beautifully like any other genuine work of art. Unity, harmony, such are the essentials of fine book building.

It became a custom among the private press printers to design their own type faces. Morris and Ricketts for example each designed three, Cobden-Sanderson at the Doves Press used only one which seemed to him able to bear the message of his books, Lucien Pissarro at the Eragny Press designed one. And with these type faces they identified themselves so thoroughly as to find their subsequent use by unknown hands an intolerable notion which must be avoided by whatever strange means. Leaving the sorts and matrices in the dustbins or burying them would only have been sordid, inadequate.

A ceremony or sacrament was needed. 'My last Will and Testament', Cobden-Sanderson announced in his journal on June 11, 1911:

10

To the Bed of the River Thames, the river on whose banks I have printed all my printed books, I bequeath The Doves Press Fount of type – the
punches, the matrices, and the type in use at the time of my death, and
may the river in its tides and flow pass over them to and from the great
sea for ever and for ever, or until its tides and flow for ever cease; then
may they share the fate of all the world, and pass from change to change
for ever upon the Tides of Time, untouched by other use and all else.

In Cobden-Sanderson this wish went far beyond the good sense of
copyright protection. One is reminded of such terrible, occasional
crimes as the nurse who murders her charges rather than let them
ever go beyond her care; or of the lady who made provision in her
will for the destruction, at her death, of the pets to which she had
been devoted. But Cobden-Sanderson was not the only one to make
sure that his beloved types could never be used by other hands. It is
worth looking at the four examples mentioned above.

The Kelmscott Press, grandest of them all, passed into the hands
of trustees when Morris died, with its secretary Sydney Cockerell in
general control. According to Cockerell's note on the history of the
press, written in 1898, Morris felt this common fear of improper use
and wished to protect his designs:

All the woodblocks for initials, ornaments, and illustrations ... have been
sent to the British Museum, and have been accepted with a condition
that they shall not be reproduced or printed from for the space of a hundred years. The electrotypes have been destroyed. In taking this course,
which was sanctioned by Morris when the matter was talked of a short
while before his death, the aim of the trustees has been to keep the series
of Kelmscott Press books as a thing apart, and to prevent the designs
becoming stale by constant repetition. Many of them have been stolen
and parodied in America, but in this country they are fortunately copy-
right. The type remains in the hands of the trustees, and will be used for
the printing of its designer's works, should special editions be called for.
Other books of which he would have approved may also be printed with
it; the absence of initials and ornament will always distinguish them sufficiently from the books printed at the Kelmscott Press.

An earlier secretary of the Press, Halliday Sparling, tells us that
Morris would never allow his type to be used for advertising pur-
poses (apart from the pamphlets and pages announcing his own
books). His spirit must be spinning in its heaven now. 'But his
refusal' Sparling writes:

raised no question as to the morality or desirability of advertising, as
things are, nor as to the duty of a printer, if he print publicity-stuff at all,
to print it as well as ever he can. It was based entirely upon another consideration, in his eyes a grave one: that the employment of given mater-

ial and a given style to advocate the buying of this or that, reduces their value and militates against their effect when they are applied to a more dignified purpose.

Then Sparling reveals his nightmare fantasy of these unknown possibilities:

> If a certain letter, for example, come to be familiarly associated with alarm-clocks or underclothing, it must necessarily be less effective when employed upon a noble poem or one of the stories or plays which count among the enduring glories of the world. Not only have its intrinsic merits been obscured, if not obliterated, by the trivialities with which the reader cannot help connecting it, but, what is worse, its lower associations reflect upon all other work in which it appears. The most enthusiastic devotee of advertising can hardly claim that it conduces to the due effect of *The Pilgrim's Progress* or *Holy Living and Dying* to read them in a type and get-up which irresistibly recalls the flavour of canned peaches, the durability of a motor-tyre, or the bargain sales of some Elite Emporium.

Of course, if Sparling's terrors were justified, more people might be reading these wise books. If the type face irresistibly recalled such delightful matters, and the steady endeavour of Christian or Faithful brought to mind some Elite Emporium, the folly of advertisement could turn back upon itself in virtue.

The Vale Press under Ricketts and Shannon lasted from 1896 until the issue of its Bibliography in 1904. In those eight years forty-six works were printed, including a complete edition of Shakespeare. The books are remembered for his arts-and-crafts ideals, a delicate use of woodcut borders, initial and illustration, and the founts of type he made for them. Both Ricketts and Shannon lived many years after the close of the Vale Press, and the reason given for closing it reads oddly: 'My reason in making this announcement was due to the fact that the number of books which were suitable to the conditions of the firm have dwindled with time.'

But it was Ricketts, writing seven years before Cobden-Sanderson's journal entry, who set the standard of action which at this distance looks so grotesque and paranoid – recording it beautifully in a page of capitals, unashamed and pre-Freud, at the opening of his Bibliography of the Vale Press:

> As it is undesirable that these founts should drift into other hands than their designers' and become stale by unthinking use, it has been decided to destroy the punches, matrices, and type with the winding up of the firm which has used them. This bibliography, therefore, contains the three founts brought together for the first and last time. The punches

and matrices are for the most part in the Thames, and on the completion of the last page of this pamphlet, the type becomes type metal again. Thus the conditions of the Vale Press are things of the past. I feel that, from the humble position of their maker, I have become part of their audience, a spectator who can applaud or blame, since the matter is at an end; my three founts have passed into the world of accomplished things, they are dead and therefore 'respectable'.

This emotional language is in the same mental world as Cobden-Sanderson, though Ricketts is not always given credit – or blamed – for getting there first. His type was already at the bottom, nobody knows where, solitary for thirteen years before the Doves type joined it. Perhaps one fell on top of the other, mixed for ever in a confusion of styles.

But the Cobden-Sanderson record becomes more complex. He considered the steps for years, and took them with elaborate embarrassment. That 'Will and Testament' from the journal reappears, his final message, at the end of the Bibliography. He was forever worrying about the gesture, and one follows its history through occasional journal entries. On a Sunday in August 1912 he wrote:

I sit in meditation on the matrices and punches of the Doves Press fount of type, and revolve in my mind whether I should destroy them in my lifetime, dedicate them to the purpose of the Press, and to the River upon whose shore the Press has lived and worked.

The chore of oblivion began in August four years later:

The Doves Press type was designed after that of Jensen; this evening I began its destruction. I threw three pages into the Thames from Hammersmith Bridge. I had gone for a stroll on the Mall, when it occurred to me that it was a suitable night and time; so I went indoors, and taking first one page and then two, succeeded in destroying three. I will now go on till I have destroyed the whole of it.

We hear from pulpits now and then that God has a sense of humour. He gently used it upon poor Cobden-Sanderson, seventy-five years old and with his hundredweights of type seeing himself in the divine image. From an evening at the end of October, 1916, we read:

I have done an extraordinary thing, which may have consequences. My object here is not only to record the fact, but my attitude to the fact. I do not mind. I rather like the idea of the discovery. I shall not attempt to hide it up if I am discovered, but shall own up and explain the object I had in view, 'to dedicate the type'. And if I am foolish, well, what can be more foolish than the whole world? My folly is of a light kind, and inexplicable by common sense, and my soul, soaring with my object, is at peace and calm, though in the actual achievement I may be thwarted. Well, what I have done is this: I went out at sundown to 'bequeath' a page of type to the 'bed of the river' – but it alighted, not on the bed of the river, but on a ledge of the far pier of the bridge, and is there now. The tide is ebbing, and there it will remain all night. Will the flow of the tide lift if off? I doubt it. But there it <u>is</u>, and now out of my reach. I aimed, and missed the bed. My idea was magnificent, the act ridiculous.

The record continues a few days later. His entry for Sunday, November the fifth, too long to be quoted adequately here, gives the adventure in magnificent detail. His fears of discovery make strange reading. What crime worried him? Anyway Ricketts had done it all before, as he must have known. Yet the fear seems to go beyond mere ridicule, and the act was always under cover of night. Those exposed packets of type on the piers of the bridge had no more criminal significance than orange peel but the thought of them appalled him:

> Imagine my consternation, and what I had to endure all that night, all Saturday and Sunday. The Thames Commissioners, the Stipendiary Magistrate, the police, the public, the newspapers! Sometimes I was desperate, and twice on Sunday, at Blenheim Road, I started to hire a boat and rescue them.

The high-minded episode becomes a hangover from school days, reported in the excitement of schoolboy language. It is not a boy but this septuagenarian mystic who lobs his load from Hammersmith bridge and daringly keeps *cave* for the police, once almost bashing it through the bottom of a boat which appeared without warning from between the arches. His secrets are packed in a box with sliding lid:

> swathed round with tape, so as to carry it like a portmanteau ... Arrived at the bridge I cross to the other side, take a stealthy look round, and if no one is in sight, I heave up the box to the parapet ... Hitherto I have escaped detection, but in the vista of coming nights I see innumerable possibilities lurking in dark corners and it will be a miracle if I escape them all.

It would be unfair to leave him without recording that the gesture was a success, and brought him peace. The needless alarms were justified. Of a July evening, the year after, he writes that his beloved river 'was another heaven, full of light from the heaven above and flooded from bank to bank – How wonderful! And my type, the Doves type was part of it! *Requiescant in pace.*

As a footnote to the story, it should be recorded that the type fount designed by Lucien Pissarro for his Eragny Press books is under the water appropriately somewhere between England and France. It was remarkably generous of Ricketts, knowing how deeply private these designs became, to allow the Vale type to be used for the first sixteen Eragny books, but in 1903 Lucien Pissarro designed his own neat and beautiful fount, known as Brook type. After Pissarro's death, and thirty years after the drowning of the Doves, his widow and son dropped it over the side of a cross-channel steamer. I asked his daughter Orovida Pissarro to tell me about this surprising episode from 1947. 'I think' she said, 'that it was very unoriginal of them'.

3

Garlands of Rachel:
The Daniel Press at Oxford

As the Daniel Press stands curiously aside from the crowded Private Press world I find some difficulty in identifying or justifying its magnetism. Many of the books are a nuisance in their overlapping paper covers which squash or tear if you push them into bookshelves. They can make attractive reading here and there in a quiet way but that might not compel the purchase of *Desiderii Erasmi Colloquia Duo*, still less the appalling poem with which Robert Bridges celebrated the end of the Boer War, called *Peace, An Ode*.

The long and peaceful life of the Reverend Charles Henry Olive Daniel, Fellow of Worcester College for fifty-three years, was not calculated to produce any great masterpiece, or even innovation, in literature or typography. His remembered achievements, the encouragement of Bridges and Richard Watson Dixon, the Fell revival, seem almost accidents: Bridges and Dixon were friends, the University Press nearby. Yet Daniel's press is a link that joins the amateur printers of an earlier age, Walpole or George Allan, with the amateurism, in a very different sense, of the Ashendene Press. It may be a backwater in the history of printing, but it has its own individual attractions. And *The Garland of Rachel*, which commemorated the first birthday of Daniel's first child (he married late) combines them all.

I appreciate the Daniel Press as I do the backwaters of the Thames, as an expression of late-Victorian Oxford. You row up the backwaters and pull under a willow to read, swim or rest where the yellow flowers of early summer, purple loosestrife and willow-herb of September decorate the banks. In those quiet places you may still see the Oxford skyline as Mrs. Daniel painted it now and then for an initial letter – St. Mary's, the Camera, All Souls, the Observatory, St. Barnabas.

Rachel's book has always been regarded as the jewel of the press, for a nice mix of reasons which appear one after the other (each inadequate) in Madan's full and affectionate description. As to its charming genesis,

> Mr. Thomas Humphry Ward made a suggestion to Dr. Daniel, presumably in 1880, that the first birthday of the latter's daughter deserved to be celebrated with special poems by his friends to be printed at the Daniel Press. Some of his friends were too diffident of their powers, some evaded the task and made delays, as the manner of writers is, but a goodly band of seventeen responded boldly to the call, and the printer-editor added one contribution himself, unsigned.

After briefly mentioning which poets liked best which poems, Madan drifts into the safer harbour of type:

> There can be no doubt that the fine typography, setting, and style of this volume, while they greatly enhanced the nascent reputation of the Press, were only secured at the cost of much care and skill. It is the first adequate specimen of the Fell type, and the first book in which large ornaments occur, to say nothing of the miniation.

As *The Garland* was printed on the small Albion press Daniel used as a boy in 1850 some difficulties and wants were experienced but

> Mrs. Daniel's free ornamentation makes up for all such needs; the capital letters in red which she supplies at the beginning of each poem are decked with tendrils which in some cases stray at will into and among the words, with beautiful effect.

Then we hear about Mr. C. M. Falconer of Dundee, whose admiration or desire was such that he made 'a special and unique transcript of the Garland, enriched with autograph letters of all the contributors, several referring to their own verses in the volume'.

Arthur Houghton owned *The Garland of Rachel* in three different forms: Falconer's manuscript, the proofs, and Robert Bridges's copy of the final printed text. Bridges was Daniel's poet, and one regrets he failed in attempting to introduce Hopkins to the Press. Instead we make do with Richard Watson Dixon, Mary Coleridge, F.W. Bourdillon and such Oxford friends as Margaret Woods and Herbert Warren, all attractive people with occasionally a good poem but not literary power-houses of the nineties. Poets of the Daniel Press deserve attention, but neither they nor Fell types are quite responsible for its character. I came away from the sale of Houghton's books with his three volumes of *The Garland*.

All of the eighteen poets who contributed received one copy with its private title page – as for instance Bridges's copy reads 'The Garland of Rachel by Robert Bridges and Divers Kindly Hands'. Those eighteen had vellum bindings over strong boards, simply and agreeably tooled in fin-de-siècle taste, unsigned but surely by Morley of Oxford. Morley (or Mrs. Daniel or Katherine Adams) were the right binders for Daniel books.

If Bridges was the poet of the Daniel Press this poem was perhaps his introduction to it, and the book Daniel's first printing of verse on his press at Oxford. They were not yet intimate friends, for Bridges addresses him as 'My Dear Sir' in a letter from London, November 1880, bound into the Houghton volume of proofs. He writes rather querulously, pleased to be asked 'But I am afraid that I cannot make a promise of this sort'. Then he threatens to complete a discarded poem in blank verse which 'will be over a hundred lines long', but changes his mind as to length, crosses out the hundred and puts '80'. It would 'require some courage to try it again', and no doubt Daniel found courage to decline. Then he goes on to canvass a notion Andrew Lang nursed, for a little book of poems on *Sleep*, English, French, Greek and perhaps Latin, but nothing came of that either. 'I'd be glad if the blank verse wd be out of the question', he adds in a postscript which probably gave the printer his escape clause.

Bridges provided a pleasant, professional, rather condensed poem of twenty-four lines for *The Garland*, in three rhyming stanzas, opening as if Blake were writing another Song of Experience:

> Press thy hands and crow,
> Thou that know'st not joy:
> Raise thy voice and weep,
> Thou that know'st not care:

It does not read like the poem of a father acquainted with his own children, and indeed he did not marry until 1884 at the age of forty. At this time he was a London doctor living in Bedford Square, the address from which he wrote so formally to Daniel. This rather creaking quality of admiration among Daniel's poets when faced with their infant subject was best expressed by Andrew Lang, married but without children:

> 'Tis distance lends, the poet says,
>   Enchantment to the view,
>   And this makes possible the praise
>   Which I bestow on you.
> For babies roseate of hue
> I do not always care,

> But distance paints the mountains blue
> And Rachel always fair.

Bridges bound into the end of his copy a far more human poem called *Rachel's Christmas Tree*, printed by Daniel in black letter two years later, but looking it up in Madan (*Oxford Minor Pieces*, 89) we find 'the verses are by Dr. Daniel himself'. Sewn into the opening of the book, wisely so nobody would remove it, is the little pamphlet called *Preface to the Garland* which each poet received but not the far-from-general public which absorbed the other eighteen Garlands, and 'few extra copies were printed', as Madan says, 'as being not relevant to the other copies. It is therefore very rare'. The printer inscribed it below, 'Worcester House, Oxford'. Bridges wrote his own name on a preliminary blank leaf of the book.

The second Houghton volume, probably bound by Mrs. Daniel, has most of the poems in various stages of proof and fifteen letters from poets to printer. Far the messiest proof is Henley's, who by writing in French caused a few problems for himself and Daniel. The theme of his amusing poem, along with several of the others, is that he cannot think what to talk to Rachel about.

> Tu ne sais rien sur le canon,
>   Rien sur l'économie antique;
> Donc parlons Darwin et guenon.
>   Nenni? Ma foi – et l'esthétique?

The little points about Henley's French are entertaining. In his small and almost equally grubby letter he asks if Daniel 'will kindly consult a big dictionary for me, & see if "Mozambique" is masculine or feminine? I haven't such a thing in the house, & I rarely go to the Museum; or I would not trouble you'. For 'guenon' in the lines above, a capital G had appeared in proof, because in another reference work Daniel must have found a Frenchman of that rather unflattering name. 'I never heard of the Guenon you have discovered', Henley writes. 'I must look him up, if it's only for curiosity's sake. My guenon, with a small g, is the ancestral she-ape, the Eve of our wretched race, the common mother of us all.'

Frederick Locker's slightly absurd *Hypnerophantasia* caused embarrassed afterthoughts in his letter of thanks to the printer, dated from Warwick Castle in November 1881. 'If I had seen the Collection before I sent you my verses I think I could have sent you something much more appropriate.' In the rough proof he had the date 1890 below his pseudo-bookish title, but Rachel aged only nine would not yet be fit recipient for such gallantry; Daniel gave her one more decade, and so it remained. This must have been Locker's second attempt, for the previous December we find Daniel's friend Willert of Exeter College discussing this contributor who seems not to have caught the mood of the book.

> 'I wrote and said the thing wouldn't do – yesterday morning's post brought me an impassioned address to Mrs. Langtrey!! which I sent back at once explaining that however great her innocence she would scarcely be considered a child. This afternoon the enclosed arrived – It seems to me pointless and I suspect does not at all meet your requirements – If I am right in determining that it won't do, would you please send it back to Locker yourself & explain why it does not suit your collection.

But Daniel was too gentle to do that. Willert rightly thought 'we are sure to get something from Courthope', but failed with 'old Henry Taylor – His wife is a great friend of mine, though I suspect the old gentleman would not care greatly to oblige me.'

When Courthope's poem is ready Willert sends it, calling him pessimist and reactionary but adding that 'with a flavour of jingoism I hope you will consider it pretty & appropriate'. Reactionary Courthope opens with the line,

> Babe, of a bitter year the early birth!

Daniel's pencil note in the proof tells us what could hardly have worried Rachel, 'general election'. And the historian of English poetry speculates as to her future.

> Born in this winter age of Loyalty,
> And Faith's decrepitude, and Art's decline?
> God sends all seasons to all things. May He
> Renew thy country's life, and perfect thine!

Humphry Ward of Brasenose, who had suggested the idea of *The Garland*, quotes in his letter to Daniel 'the charming Miss Robinson' who seems to have discussed with him her contribution and to have hit the nail on the head by saying 'Here is a lullaby which I have written to Baby Rachel – so you must measure it by her standard of appreciation & not by yours'. Mary Robinson's poem, admired apparently by Symonds, may not live in the anthologies but at least she thought of Rachel instead of adapting awkwardly to a theme beyond customary range. In another letter Ward passes on a message from Gosse who wanted to write a brief review, and if Scribner the New York publisher were allowed to reproduce one of Alfred Parsons's flowery decorations 'a cry of joyous gratitude would rise to heaven from the office'. Ward contributes a pleasant poem, wishing Rachel

> A head that's tolerably quick,
>   And that the imperious sway
> Of Grammar and Arithmetic
>   Will not too much dismay.

It seems Andrew Lang's friendship came earlier than that of Bridges, and that he helped Daniel towards acquaintance with the poets; for *The Garland* is a mixture, as the Press would be, of Oxford friends and the outer world of poetry. As to their presence together in 1881, 'Mr. Symonds remarks', according to Madan, 'that the unprofessional poets were good'. Lang himself feels 'almost as bad at writing on a given topic, as at algebra. Gosse, on the other hand, is very clever at it. I only know Bridges, who strikes the chorded shell, beside Gosse and Dobson, but if I make acquaintance with a poet, I will entreat his aid. Perhaps Miss Mary Robinson or O'Shaughnessy could send a stanza or two ...' And from him the printer receives Henley's French piece.

Gosse became a good friend to Daniel and his press, editing one book and owning most. One may come upon his copies now and then. The poem he offered seems now among the best, though it had no votes in Madan's list. Gosse had views about Daniel's use of the archaic long 's', and got his way in the printing of his own name but not in the poem which he similarly corrected. The first of two letters from him is worth quoting, dated from London in February 1881:

My Dear Sir,

  I have no corrections to make in the proof which you have been so good as to send me. I should be glad if my name might have short s's instead of long ones. There was an Elizabethan poetaster called Goffe.

  My poor friend Arthur O'Shaughnessy designed a contribution to the "Garland of Rachel", but his sudden death has made it impossible to find out whether he had or had not written it. His executor tells me that he finds no such poem among his MSS.

  I am looking forward with much pleasure to the volume, which will be exquisite in its material part, at all events.

                    Yours very faithfully
                    Edmund W. Gosse

The awkward slope of Austin Dobson's hand, from the Board of Trade in March 1881, introduces a charming poem which all

Madan's voters included among their favourites. Even he was as worried as most of them by addressing a one-year-old girl:

> What rocks there are on either hand!
>   Suppose – 'tis on the cards –
> You should grow up with quite a grand
>   Platonic hate for bards!
>
> How shall I then be shamed, undone,
>   For ah! with what a scorn
> Your eyes must greet that luckless One
>   Who rhymed you, newly born;
>
> Who o'er your 'helpless cradle' bent
>   His idle verse to turn;
> And twanged his tiresome instrument
>   Above your unconcern!

Nobody would particularly remember Lewis Carroll for his poem in *The Garland*, though some know *The Garland* because it includes his poem. Apart from a couple of lines about the lark it is best ignored, yet it is followed by *Idem Latine Redditum* by a baronet, Sir Richard Harington of Whitbourne Court, Worcester. The little poem was really not worth so much labour or attention to detail, but Harington writes to Daniel an earnest formal letter in the third person about his Latin rendering of Lewis Carroll.

> He must apologise for the delay which his (after all very unsuccessful) attempt to render Dodgson's lines into Latin worthy of them must already have caused.
>   But his version which was he must admit very full indeed of faults in the first instance has been subjected to a good deal of criticism by Mr. Onions, as these could only be answered or obviated by a reference to authorities, & as Sir Richard Harington's time is very closely occupied ...

Busy Sir Richard follows Lewis Carroll in the book, which one views with a new sense of Daniel's art after time spent upon these proofs and in the Victorian handwriting of contributors.

So we have looked at most of the poems in Houghton's volume of proofs, with related letters, and it ends with an envelope which holds *Preface to the Garland*. With a printed letter to his authors Daniel introduces a marvellous passage about infancy by Bishop Earle, writing in the seventeenth century, 'which I still cannot refuse myself the pleasure of recalling to your memory'. He mentions that 'the whole of the Printer's work has been done by myself, the miniation by my Wife; the Printer's mark and the head-pieces are a contribution of Mr. Alfred Parsons.'

We come to the remarkable volume written out and assembled by Mr. C. M. Falconer of Dundee, as Madan tells us, third of the Houghton Garlands. Falconer was an Andrew Lang collector, so we can expect strength there, but he took much trouble to make this a delightful book, seeking letters and signatures from each poet and getting the assembly bound appropriately by Zaehnsdorf. The letters, mounted on guards, extend to the outer margins.

After writing out his book (as Daniel had told him an original would be 'introuvable') Falconer risked it in the post about sixteen times to get the poets to sign and favour him with a letter. Often it worked, some would only sign, others were too withdrawn even to do that. Daniel helped out if he could. The result is an idiosyncratic volume of some charm, a tale of mystery and imagination, adding letters where none existed in Houghton II, evidence of one bibliophile's devotion.

Falconer's homage is quite mysterious. With half-title and dedication his printer managed creditable type-facsimile, not using Daniel's Dutch handmade paper. The Misit mark and Alfred Parsons's flowery woodcuts must have been traced, not photographed. Very small differences are detectable, so he did not borrow the blocks. His own handwriting is undistinguished, but he dared to imitate Mrs. Daniel's trailing red initial letters; so the poets saw a creditable labour of love, adding to it their signatures and letters. His endeavour was gracefully blessed by Daniel in a letter dated from Worcester College, 23 December 1896, in which he wrote:

Dear Sir,

I herewith return to you by Registered Parcel your very admirable transcript of the 'Garland of Rachel' – you have done the Book too much honour in taking such pains over it. If my printed copies are a treasure to the collector, your MS is ten times more so. And the copies of the head pieces are perfect – while your printer has caught the look of the somewhat artless volume quite admirably.

I am sorry to have kept it so long, but I lay in ambush for the one or two Oxford contributors – to obtain their signatures for you – Alas! I have been able to do next to nothing for you. Two – 'W' and Lewis Carroll would not be won over. The former from modesty, the latter because even in this case he would not break his rule – never to give his signature. Mrs. Woods I got upon her return to Oxford and your humble servant has signed a

production of his own for the first time. So that I am not quite re
infecta.

But to atone to some extent for this failure I have hunted up
and send for your acceptance a copy of the missive which was
despatched to each of the authors with his copy – I doubt if I have
another of these myself.

With best Xmas wishes

I am

Yours faithfully

C Henry Daniel

Daniel thus provides a key to several parts of this volume, beginning with yet another copy of the rare *Preface to the Garland* and following by a signature of his own poem which strikes nearer to
infancy than most:

> Rachel! babe, whose frolic smile
> Might a stoic's frown beguile,
> Thou small quintessential thing,
> That does heaven to mortals bring ...

A family ending to *The Garland* may also be mentioned here, the
final poem by Daniel's Cruttwell uncle whose sonnets he had printed
as a boy at Frome. Cruttwell being dead, Daniel sent his signature
and Falconer stuck it below this sonnet, adding an amusing note in
the accompanying letter:

> "Lewis Carroll" – the Rev. C. Dodgson, Christ Church Oxford – you
> might try, but I do not think for a moment you will overcome his
> resolution never under any circumstances to give his autograph. I appre-
> hend he will even take a sort of pleasure in being the only blank.

Falconer netted them all, with the printer's help, Watson and
Dodgson proving most difficult. 'What odd forms modesty takes',
writes Daniel, ' – as in Mr. Watson's case. It is with him pure
bashfulness, not as with Dodgson – a caprice.' But Dodgson died
in 1897, and at the end of the next January Falconer received from
the printer a generous note: 'I enclose you a holograph of our
lamented friend – of some interest in itself – to which you are
welcome'.

So they got him in the end, with a delightful letter to Mrs. Daniel
(stamped envelope also bound in), fussy and characteristic, telling
her not to leave things in envelopes because they might get lost,
going on to describe his old-fashioned method with the camera and
its merits:

I suppose you have taken to the 'dry' process. I wish some amateur would again take up the 'wet' process, which I worked for 25 years. Its results are far more delicate and artistic ... I would take it up again myself, if I could, but expect the rest of my life will be none too much for the writing I have yet to do.

Mrs. Daniel, in sending some 'printed verses', had enclosed a note offering a photograph of her two daughters Rachel and Ruth.

They also caught Watson of Brasenose somewhat unfairly by binding in his letter of refusal. 'I am afraid that the reasons which have led me to decline hitherto to allow my name to appear among those of the contributors to "the Garland of Rachel" are still in force.' Bashful Albert Watson, Fellow of Brasenose, author of four Latin lines in *The Garland*, 'was found dead in bed yesterday morning' in November 1904. 'He attended the University Church on Sunday morning, but was greatly upset later in the day when he heard of the death of Dr. Fowler, President of Corpus Christi, who was a very old friend of his'. Watson had been Fellow of Brasenose more than half a century.

Austin Dobson simply signed his piece for Falconer, but Lang gave his admirer three stanzas of a new poem ('Red roses under the sun') which are bound in, with Falconer's note below: 'Received 8th January 1897 from Mrs. Andrew Lang at St. Andrews in my MS copy of The Garland of Rachel'.

John Addington Symonds was dead but Gosse dependably sent his signature, mounted now below the poem, with a flattering letter:

> Your transcript of the Garland of Rachel is a miracle of skilful and industrious ingenuity. I would fain add something to such a labour of love, and I therefore enclose the signature of my dear late friend, Mr. Symonds.

Bridges signed, and the Worcester baronet wrote his elaborate embarrassment about two blunders in the Latin version of Lewis Carroll's poem due to an unfortunate circumstance: 'Unluckily he by mistake printed from the wrong M.S. & I don't like to affirm blunders which I had endeavoured to correct'. All very awkward but they find a way out: 'It seems to me that the best way out of the difficulty will be to append footnotes in ink, as & when I have written them in lead pencil'. The device is followed, Falconer's ink emendations follow Sir Richard's instructions.

Then we find a flurry of Mary Robinson, and Gosse himself. Gosse helps in the hunt, explaining 'Miss Mary Robinson is the widow of the late Prof. Darmesteter and lives in Paris', providing the address of her mother whose long and dotty reply is also bound in.

Mrs. Darmesteter worries about receiving such a precious parcel in her travels, so her poem goes unsigned but Gosse gives instead an amusing and diffident letter from her, 'When I was Vice President of the little Debating Soc: at University College the Students used to say "Miss Robinson then arose & said a very few words & all in one syllable" '.

As to two other evasive contributors, Gosse wrote in January 1897 that he knew 'nothing of Mr. Bourdillon, and Mr. Ernest Myers (I believe) lives somewhere in the country'. To Bourdillon, doubly a Daniel Press poet, Falconer was no doubt directed by the printer and he signed, quite a charming poem from which it might be unkind to quote lines out of context. Henley and Courthope send courteous notes and sign. Humphry Ward felt 'much flattered by the tribute you have paid to the little volume, of which I believe I was the first to give the suggestion to Mr. Daniel', and signed. Ernest Myers, late in the book, was one of the last to be asked. Falconer sent the whole parcel to them all, not just their own pages. 'From what I remember of the signatures', Myers remarks in the second of two letters on black-bordered mourning paper, 'I trust that its journeys & your consequent anxieties are nearly or quite over'. His two slight verses record of his stern Lyre that

> the tiny finger of a child
> Had touched – no more – the string.

Margaret Woods, back in Oxford, signed as Daniel had said. Her poem, one of the longest, called *Little Gilbert Speaks* (I am ignorant as to why it was so named) beginning

> Rachel! tell me what you know,
> Tell me where the shadows go,

is the pleasant if sentimental fantasy of one who saw Rachel in her mind's eye and knew the family. Three appalling lines from his great-uncle Cruttwell's sonnet conclude *The Garland of Rachel*:

> Dear little Rachel, as we pray,
> Precious ewe-lamb, and sprinkle, we discern
> The heavenly Jacob's arms, which thee engird.

So we close the three Houghton books, and rise for our pigeon's-eye view of Rachel's garland after a century. Its attraction is difficult to isolate – several agreeable poems, rarity, an enchanting idea, first editions; but more than these, Oxford's welcome to an infant when poets saw little of children, whether they had them or not, and struggled to imagine how contact might be made in a few lines. Warren of

Magdalen, a Daniel poet, wrote in his Memoirs, 1921, 'That cradle-crowning of Rachel provided the cradle-crowning of the Daniel Press. The first important production, and in some ways still the most striking, as it is one of the rarest, of that Press, *Rachel's Garland* becomes the precursor of the fair and rare series which has enriched the libraries of two generations and both shores of the Atlantic'.

4

Print and Design in Eighteenth-Century Editions of Shakespeare

Shakespeare folios, ugly and desirable, appeared in each quarter of the seventeenth century but the eighteenth-century idea came with a difference. Nobody had prepared, before, a pleasant production: small volumes with a preface, illustrations, the courtesy and manners which belong in libraries. These were the earliest Shakespeare sets, first agreeable editions, and they formed a history from Rowe's six volumes in 1709 to the Boswell–Malone variorum of 1821 in twenty-one volumes, 'the foundation', as everyone agreed, 'of modern Shakespeare scholarship'.

Feeling no warmth for modern Shakespeare scholarship I welcome the finality of 1821. Within those dates had grown the debates, among a succession of editors: Rowe, Pope, Theobald, Hanmer, Warburton, Johnson, Capell, Steevens, Reed, Malone. They, after the two actors who put the first folio together, have given us Shakespeare. That was the birth for better or worse of Eng. Lit. Crit. No author, writing in English, had had each phrase teased out for meaning before Theobald shouldered – with much pleasure – that task. All were strong characters, Rowe the poet laureate first on the scene stepping into hot water without knowing its temperature.

They disputed points of reference, of sense, omissions and corruptions, with each other; stretched the debate in print as it rose from the foot of a page almost to fill it. Try the difficult first scene of *Measure for Measure*, as it appears in Rowe and then in the 1821 variorum, three pages stretching to fourteen. Nobody hesitated to print his pre-

28

decessor's notes, in order to knock them on the head. Johnson was especially harsh in concise demolition of Warburton. Steevens, temperamental and brilliant, enjoyed mischief and created it. Pope fought with Theobald, Warburton with Hanmer; Malone brought an excess of sobriety, but his was not the first twenty-one volume edition.

Within this whole scheme, incidental to it, one may view a spectrum of English printing, illustration and book design, from humdrum to the heights. As publications of Shakespeare proliferated during the century and after, I confine this discussion to such as are of interest editorially, typographically, or for their engravings. Within that limit it must be agreed that the editors who set up as scholars to advance our close understanding of the plays, in the first half of this period, were Theobald, Warburton and Johnson; and it is conspicuously true that first editions of all three were, as to design, entirely humdrum and average for their time – readable and acceptable in their old calf bindings but with no thought to rise above a certain level (or fall below it). To mention a technical point, headlines on both sides of the page in all three give only the play's title: no helpful mention of act and scene, for ease of reference. The second edition of Theobald (1740) received attractive illustrations, but those three were unadorned presences. This could be reckoned a descent from the first 'library edition', Rowe's of 1709, which shows no particular art of printing but was, like Theobald's thirty years later, pleasantly illustrated.

It would be commonly true, though Capell was an exception, that eighteenth-century Shakespeares which focus upon new editorial work compensated by neglecting graceful design. The general truth continues through successive versions by Johnson and Steevens, Reed, Malone – though one neglected labourer, Blair, professor of rhetoric, better known for printing his dull sermons, offered something better in the Edinburgh publication of 1755. Small innovations appeared – act and scene references among the headlines – and all had their passions, prejudices, learning and debate but they cannot be shown as models of book art.

It was not through any lack of knowledge, or the absence of public taste for a fine book. Pope always cared about the printing of his work: Pope's edition, 1723–5, marks the first advance towards splendour in treatment of a Shakespeare text, and Hanmer's (1743–5) the second. As both of them had, and have retained, a poor reputation editorially, the general rule seems to be confirmed that attention to design advances as attention to text recedes. Pope's edition and Hanmer's are handsome quartos. Pope made sure his Shakespeare was not inferior to the Homer which had preceded it; Hanmer wanted his Shakespeare to seem finer than Pope's, making a great point about having paid the artist and offered his text to Oxford without fee. Neither seems especially marvellous now, but they were the first Shakespeares which aimed in the direction of fine printing; on good paper, the Hanmer edition illustrated with Hayman's designs engraved by Gravelot[1].

The history of ordinary – *characteristic* is a better word – book-production could be continued and extended. Stockdale's one-volume edition (the first octavo single-volume Shakespeare, 1784) was an appalling affair, his extension of it in three volumes a few years later not much better. German eighteenth-century editions – for instance the Manheim publication of 1779 – did not rise above common level; but it is just to add that the first French translations of Shakespeare, in eight volumes under the general title *Le Theatre Anglois* (1746) were no less elegant, with their assemblies of decoration from printers' flowers, than one would expect in French books of the period.

Rather than linger in analysis of the expected and the second-rate, one is drawn towards whatever was exceptional and excellent in eighteenth-century Shakespeare – and more especially, because little attention has been given to this aspect of a subject which deserves it. For a start, those who enjoy large-paper sets may find them here, and they are worth seeking. Rowe on large paper may well be distinguished as the first bibliophile printing of Shakespeare; Theobald (1733) on large paper is an eccentric and wonderful production; Bell on large paper is perhaps the most refined and perfect among eighteenth-century versions – I refer to the twenty volumes from 1786–8, which use the Johnson–Steevens text and notes, not to the early Bell publication in nine volumes (1775) of which copies were also issued on large paper but printing the altered text used in theatres. And there are large-paper sets of the Johnson–Steevens edition of 1793, in fifteen volumes, printed by Baldwin.

I want to pause among these, but it is not commonly recognised – because the printing of Shakespeare as art has been neglected – that editions from the eighteenth century exist in the types of Baskerville, from the Foulis Press, from Bulmer and Bensley and Bell. As a bibliophile feast there was no lack of provision.

Rowe on large paper is a splendid event, if you like large-paper copies. The subject is not frivolous. Good margins give a sense of

---

[1] A couple were also drawn by Gravelot, in much the same style, apparently because Hayman found difficulty in completing them in time to be paid according to contract.

occasion in the reading; common margins in the eighteenth century were often poor, less than adequate; and the large copies were always printed on better paper. Opening a volume of large-paper Rowe at random, it provides apt lines from the start of Act V, *The Tempest*:

> Now does my Project gather to a head:
> My Charms crack not; my Spirits obey, and Time
> Goes upright with his Carriage.

That sets the scene for pleasure in reading, which stands higher for those who prefer Shakespeare on the page, than extravagant scenery on stage. The two are comparable.

A spurious seventh volume, issued by Curll to look as if it belonged to Rowe's edition – 'Volume the Seventh' says the title page – appeared in 1710. Curll also issued his 'seventh volume' on large paper. The binder of my large-paper volume seven had also bound the smaller version, creating for both a large dianthus at the corners of panels on all four covers. With decent margins the illustrations, of course, are easier to appreciate.

The magnificent surprise of Theobald on large paper is partly from its thickness, the paper of quite different character; and generous margins, as ever, change the experience of reading. As Rowe and Theobald were the two most important pioneering editors – Rowe first of all, Theobald providing the first detailed critical edition of an English author – 'literal criticism' he called it – those bibliophile versions of both transport their pleasures across nearly three centuries.

Margins may deceive, in an uncut copy. In France the folding of sheets, at a later date than this, was sometimes deliberately erratic, giving an emphatic – false – appearance to uncut copies; but from accident rather than purpose one finds a similar habit often among English eighteenth-century binders. Thus uncut volumes may look like large-paper, when set beside the same work conventionally trimmed and bound. Comparing two sets of the 1785 Johnson–Steevens–Reed Shakespeare, one after normal trimming in contemporary calf, the other quite uncut in a later binding of parchment over boards, a temptation to call the uncut set large-paper has, I *think*, to be resisted.

Theobald's thickness and depth banish all doubt, in this set which survives as it would have been seen in the bookshop: marbled paper over boards, sheepskin backs, hand-written title labels. Contemporary calf of an ordinary set, which overlaps the pages, is seven and three-quarter inches high; boards of the large-paper set, same size as the pages, are ten inches high. The large (and largely unpressed) set is three-quarters of an inch thicker, measuring the same volume, than in the normal set.

These two (Rowe, Theobald) count as intellectual editions of which the publisher chose to print a few on large paper. Most of the intellectual editions offered no such gesture: Warburton, Johnson, none of the Johnson–Steevens revisions until 1793, nothing of the sort from Malone (1790). The exception was Bell, as publisher, with his twenty volumes issued between 1786 and 1788.

Bell used the Johnson–Steevens text, with skill and panache. As his normal-edition format was small, pocket-size, notes were for the first time printed separately at the back. Binders often treated the Bell Shakespeare rather ignorantly, making separate volumes for the notes, throwing out title pages, confusing illustrations, muddling the two volumes of Prolegomena. Perhaps for these reasons the twenty-volume Shakespeare has been neglected as an endeavour in publishing, though Stanley Morison wrote about Bell's types, and his modern use of s has been well recognised. As a publishing-cum-editorial achievement (though that is not the point of this essay) it strikes me as the most considerable Shakespeare to have been issued up to that time.

As to sets on large paper, nowhere could their advantage be more clearly shown. Bell's clear types, his taste (and the engravings) give great charm to this pocket edition; on large paper it is transformed. The *quality* of paper in such sets is marvellous – hot-pressed, I would guess. First-rate printing upon such paper, without blemish of blot or show-through, and with a sense of leisure from the margins, produces the finest artistic result among all the many eighteenth-century versions. This set in tree-calf from that time is as near perfect as one could hope; experience of reading is influenced by condition, but if judging by artistic standards I would vote for Bell. Comparable sets in contemporary binding, ordinary and large-paper, are respectively five and three-quarter inches high, and seven and a half inches.

One must not confuse (it has been done in distinguished company) this edition which is admirable from every angle, with the nine volumes issued by Bell in 1773–5. In illustration the treatment was similar (from particular productions, as interpreted by the actors named) but the earlier version printed the plays 'as they are now performed at the Theatres Royal in London', a far cry from Johnson–Steevens. I have not seen large-paper copies; they exist, some distance from Shakespeare.

The last among these undoubted large-paper examples, Johnson and Steevens in fifteen volumes (1793) appeared with more conscious care for design than had been evident in earlier scholarly editions – except those of Pope and Hanmer, whose texts lie outside the borders of modern acceptance. That 1793 edition was a dramatic event, for which Steevens worked non-stop to oppose and replace Malone's edition of 1790; returning to the field from retirement, stimulated by a footnote squabble with Malone. As ever, in these serious initiatives, the text was unadorned. 'We boast therefore of no exterior ornaments', he wrote, 'except those of better print and paper than have hitherto been allotted to any octavo edition of Shakespeare'. Perhaps in that limited claim he had in mind the second Hanmer edition, issued by Oxford in 1771 with balanced margins, large quarto as before, on admirable paper.

The claim was proper, these are handsome and careful books; the printer was Baldwin, one of many who could produce excellent work though their names and his are not chosen above others, as are Bulmer and Bensley, for particular study. As to large paper, the first volume here has the following inscription:

> This set of Shakespeare's plays in Fifteen Vols. Royal 8vo, of which only 25 Copies were taken off on that Large sized Paper, was presented to me by its Editor Mr. George Steevens, in consideration of the care with which I superintended its entire progress through my Father's Press.

And below that he has added:

> I give to my Dear Daughter Mary Sophia Chenevix.
> Charles Baldwin
> Nov. 10th 1859.

The time span is remarkable, but not impossible. Making the gift sixty-six years after seeing these books responsibly through the press, he must then have been well into his eighties. He had them bound for his dear daughter, by R. Hastings of Carey Street, Lincoln's Inn, who trimmed and marbled the edges so that it seems not now to be so very large; but margins remain satisfactory, and paper rather stronger than was used for the edition.

My only other large-paper contribution, to be mentioned before this subject becomes really tedious, is the 1807 quarto edition, printed for Stockdale by Bensley, commonly called Heath's because he made some engravings for it after paintings by Stothard. Stockdale, enterprising and opportunist, produced this splendid reply – it could not be less than excellent, with Bensley's eye and art – to the Boydell folios printed a few years before by Bulmer. Large-paper sets of this large quarto edition are not mentioned by Jaggard, but they exist. Mine is a curious compilation, owned once by (and presumably bound for) Sir William Gore Ouseley, who managed to find many of the plays on large paper but not all. No skill was needed to detect that history, for he had the sense to get them bound uncut; so one sees the deckle edges of ordinary and large paper within the same binding – according to which plays were available, one supposes, on large paper when he wanted them, and which were not. Some have been extended to large-paper size, with less happy result. The binder was rather strong than artistic. This mélange is extra-illustrated and at Stratford there exists a set extended to double its length.

Art should bear no relation to size, among the vast majority of right-minded people – and yet, and yet ... Among the smaller, well-designed Shakespeares none stands out as a conscious claimant before Capell's edition, 1767–8, published by Tonson, printed in a style quite different from its predecessors by Dryden Leach who was oddly described by Nichols in *Literary Anecdotes* as 'the father of *Fine Printing* in this Country'. If that phrase these days brings overtones of bombast and excess, they existed also in the eighteenth century; but 'clean and decent' strikes me as more apt for Dryden Leach, whose work should probably be investigated; he has not struck through to articles in journals by the type-obsessed. As Capell's Shakespeare follows the manner of his *Prolusions* printed by Leach in 1759, and his neat quarto manuscripts in the Wren Library at Cambridge were written in the same pattern – down to the detail of an open rectangle above each new play or chapter – it seems likely Capell asked the printer to follow closely the scheme of his manuscript. We know he liked clean pages, undamaged by footnotes, 'that a very great part of the world, amongst whom is the editor himself, profess much dislike to this paginary intermixture of text and comment'; and no doubt he requested such margins as make a normal set seem as if it was printed on large paper.

In this better-than-usual vein of clarity with neatness I would place the two Scottish versions: Blair's Edinburgh edition (1753) and the curiously rare Foulis Press Shakespeare (1752–66). The Edinburgh edition is called 'first Scottish', because it was completed in 1753, though the Foulis Press version, appearing in parts across fourteen years, has 1752 on the title pages of its first two plays, *The Tempest* and *A Midsummer Night's Dream*. The relevant point here is that they compare in character and quality, except that in Glasgow Pope's text was chosen: 'Collated and Corrected by the former Editions, by Mr. Pope' who had died in 1744. Warburton had not established himself, Hanmer was not well received, they could have used Theobald notorious from the *Dunciad*.

From the textual standpoint one prefers the Edinburgh edition, which made no claim upon new scholarship but picked and chose the work of successive editors through the first half-century. Blair, after summarising it, wrote in 'The Scots Editors Preface' as it was called:

> Amidst such a variety of editors, and such different characters of them, no one could be implicitly followed. We have therefore consulted them all; and, of the various readings and conjectures, those only have been adopted, and inserted in the text, that seemed to agree best with the meaning of the author.

And though that reads like a slack and self-indulgent form of editing, the result is better than Pope's. So I would choose Blair, if I were to read Shakespeare this morning, Edinburgh rather than Glasgow, though both have equal merit as inking and printing in small octavo. Gaskell calls the Foulis Press paper 'medium-poor quality', but Theobald and Warburton were worse. Scrupulous work can cope with medium paper. It is worth adding that Dodd's *Beauties of Shakespear*, appearing in 1752, was much quoted by Blair in his preface and may also have influenced the design of his edition. Dodd is more often remembered as a forger who was hanged, than for this youthful example of promise and ambition.

The Martin brothers, Robert and William, were conspicuous in the late-eighteenth century English typographic revival. Robert Martin, manager at Baskerville's plant in Birmingham, took charge when the great man was away or inactive from nervous depression, during which several works were produced under his own supervision. One such period coincided with Garrick's plans for the chaotic Shakespeare Jubilee celebrations, for which Martin using Baskerville's types produced his set in nine small octavo volumes (1768) 'With Notes selected from the best Authors, Explanatory, and Critical', but again using Pope's text. It was perhaps early for him to have known the merits of Johnson's. In fact there were very few notes of any sort, no prefaces or glossary; this is not a distinguished edition except that it must rank as Baskerville's. I suppose no Shakespeare plays had been printed, before these, so close to Stratford! In the types, occasional ornament and a habit of spacing, Baskerville is detectable. It is not an edition commonly seen. Margins in my copy are less than generous.

Boydell's Shakespeare, issued in parts during the last decade of the century, was beyond challenge the most splendid accomplishment: born of an idea thrown out during a dinner party of publishers and artists in Hampstead, expanding to become a great gallery of paintings illustrating scenes from Shakespeare, engraved then for the printed edition; engraved also on very large copper plates – wider yet and wider shall thy bounds be set – for vast folios known generally, like the place itself, as the Shakespeare Gallery, whose portico survives in the garden of New Place at Stratford. The nine tall folios, text without notes, exhibited Bulmer's printing together with the gallery's art and Boydell's aspiration. The Boydell Shakespeare stands among several such monuments of folio book-production from that decade, printed by Bulmer or Bensley: Hume's *History of England*, Macklin's *Bible*, Boydell's *Milton*.

From the same period of admirable English printing came other able editions of Shakespeare, less bombastic than that of Boydell. Among them one thinks especially of Harding's edition – so named on the title pages, twelve small-octavo volumes issued in parts during the last two years of the century. Harding, not commonly remembered, got Bensley to print them, with prefaces but no notes, 'Accurately Printed from the text of Mr. Steevens's Last Edition'; with a new set of stipple engravings and on good paper, so that a bookseller could write in my copy: '124 copper plates without foxing'. If this comes from the Glasgow–Edinburgh–Birmingham tradition, minor evidence of Bensley's art in using rules, open lettering for titles, Bewick's wood engraving of a swan on the general title page, lifts it a little higher. For the first quarter of the nineteenth century a form of neo-classical good taste had arrived.

One other set, not particularly well printed though the attempt was made, forces its way into this quick tour: eight volumes published by Bellamy and Robarts in 1791. The gothic scheme of illustration, so different and original, undertaken three and four years before the books appeared, transforms this into an astonishing production.

As my purpose was to view the spectrum of printing through these many editions of the plays, and we have so far travelled from average to excellent, a dip into one of the worst is appropriate though it raises impossible questions as to what seems desirable: the 'first American Edition' (title-page phrase), 'corrected from the latest and best London editions, with notes, by Samuel Johnson, L.L.D.', eight small-octavo volumes, appeared at Philadelphia in 1795. This venture was important for more than Shakespeare, opening a vein of locally printed 'Collected Works'; American publishers saw no particular need, after this, to import them from England. But it was printed on poor paper, which has acquired a regular pattern of brown-blotching across two centuries. This set, with the book-plates of Henry Irving, has been elaborately re-backed; I like to think his common use of it made such treatment necessary.

The awkward question is Marlowe's, 'What asketh man to have?' Here are fine printing (tiresome phrase) on excellent paper, and these blotched American firsts – seen thus also in another, far more presentable set, which had not been re-backed (nor had it belonged to Irving). I leave the debate without voting. The finest Japanese manuscripts were often written on patterned or painted papers. It has seemed to me that the effect of pale brown marbling over all this paper from Philadelphia is not unlike those Japanese designs; that the plays are quite readable above it, an organic and politically correct experience.

It is interesting to note how few among so many editions offered the simple convenience, in the headlines, of act and scene numbers. These were not provided before the Edinburgh and Glasgow editions; Blair and the Foulis Press appearing across the same years, perhaps there was a little industrial spying. The 1803 variorum offered no such help, nor had any of the scholarly editions (except Blair's), but it entered the 1813 twenty-one volume reprint and was again used in the Boswell–Malone variorum of 1821. The only others to earn honourable mention in this regard are Bell, Harding, and the maligned Philadelphia edition, which each gave references to acts but not scenes. In looking for particular passages this neglect is always a nuisance, witness to the great divide between printer and user.

5

John Baptist Jackson and Chiaroscuro

Jackson, an energetic innovating Englishman, belonged to no period but was born with the eighteenth century. His voice is in the strange and rather brilliant publication from 1754, *An Essay on the Invention of Engraving and Printing in Chiaro Oscuro, as practised by Albert Durer, Hugo Di Carpi &c. and the Application of it to the Making Paper Hangings of Taste, Duration, and Elegance, by Mr. Jackson, of Battersea. Illustrated with Prints in proper Colours.* There he declares, of the art he had chosen, that 'though those delicate Finishings, and minute Strokes, which make up great Part of the Merit of engraving on Copper, are not to be found in those cut on Wood in Chiaro Oscuro; yet there is a masterly and free Drawing, a Boldness of Engraving and Relief, which pleases a true Taste more than all the little Exactness found in the Engravings on Copper Plates'.

He was not a man for 'the little exactness', and I find that a sympathetic quality. An excellent book on Jackson was written fourteen years ago by Jacob Kainen, who discovered few details of the man beyond his art. 'If he does not emerge from this study', Kainen wrote, 'completely accounted for from birth to death, it has not been because of lack of effort. Biographical data for his early and late life – about fifty years in all – are almost entirely missing despite years of diligent search'. The Battersea authorities, to my slight relief, could find no trace and offered no encouragement.

So we may think more freely of what Jackson attempted, the tradition he inherited and where he stood in his time. In all this I have no 'little exactness' to offer, of detailed biography or printing method, and he would not too much have minded the omission. We

38

tend these days to focus upon Bewick, and the extreme finesse of wood engraving in the eighteen-sixties. Jackson, trained and strained in the precision of Paris, stayed true to his temperament of knife and plank. As he put it:

> In this manner of doing Prints in Chiaro Oscuro, when the Out-line is just (and which Mr. Jackson presumes those Gentlemen will be inclined to allow him who shall be pleased to honour his Performance with the least Attention) the Impression resembles a Drawing more than any other Way in which Prints are done, and indeed has an Effect which the best Judges very often prefer to any Prints from Engravings, done with all the Exactness, minute Strokes of the Graver, and Neatness of Work, which is sure to captivate the Minds of those whose Taste is form'd upon the little Considerations of delicately handling the Tools, and not upon the Freedom, Life and Spirit of the separate Figures, and indeed the whole Composition.

Every engraving attempts to interpret light and shade, chiaro and oscuro. The problem may be solved by density of line, and cross-hatching; or by variety in back-ground texture, as with the dotted woodcut, white on black, called criblé, looking like perpetual snow-storm; or, half a century before Jackson started, by the rocking and scraping of mezzotint. This use of printed colour to interpret pictures – a more direct form of translation than cross-hatching – dates from the start of the sixteenth century, but colour in its wider sense of tone or texture is just the endeavour of any age towards greater sophistication than simple outline. The notion of black-and-white engraving to interpret a painting is nearer the purity of inventive art, than colour-printing which leans towards visual imitation; but that step in logic, applicable perhaps to photography, was far away from the work of Ugo da Carpi.

The technical ingenuity of red and blue and black, as in the Mainz Psalter, and colour used in diagrams to illustrate Hyginus or the Book of St. Albans, has nothing to do with the interpretation or reproduction of paintings. One fascination of chiaroscuro is that it could never attempt a very close imitation – could never become fac-simile. In Holland a little after Jackson's day Ploos van Amstel used to stamp the back of each published print with his own device, so that nobody would mistake it for the original drawing or accuse him of forgery. But the marvellous work of Ploos, replete with 'little exactness', was far from Jackson.

Julia Frankau, in an able and neglected book on colour printing, defined chiaroscuro as 'successive printings from a series of wood blocks; the first block carrying the outlines and deep shadows, and the following ones the broad effects of light, shade and colour'. The relief printed tone blocks would commonly be cut so as to let white highlights from the paper itself show through. Two sorts of chiaroscuro developed during the sixteenth century in Germany and Italy. The German school, including Lucas Cranach and Hendrik Goltzius, a Dutchman, tended to use more precise outline with white highlights through a single tone background. In Italy a manner developed at once more free and perhaps better suited to plank-wood interpretation of colour.

As the word comes to us from Italy, so the Italian chiaroscuri show a bravery in concept which takes them apart from all other kinds of interpretative print. The strong shadows and brushlike drawing of Ugo da Carpi, working in the few years before 1520, could achieve the spontaneity of a studio sketch. One common quality of Italian work was this nearness to the artist himself. Antonio da Trento is known to have done much in the studio of Parmigianino, and under his supervision. I am grateful to a calligraphic friend, Madeleine Dinkel, whose eye and knowledge of the tools suggested at once, examining a few examples, that those broad shadow outlines must have been made upon the wood by such a reed as the artist used for his original drawing; and what more likely, working so close, than that the artist made the first sketches or at least assisted the wood-cutter with them? Similar studio partnerships existed between Guido Reni and Coriolano, for instance, in the early seventeenth century; or between Büsinck, the first to take this method into France, and L'Allemand, a German artist working there.

We have to recall that print world of the sixteenth century: hundreds of etchers and engravers in black and white, all the outline elegance of woodcut from Lyons, the emblems and the allegories, and just these few – to be counted on the fingers of two hands probably – enjoying their colour experiments in Italy. Starting as outsiders, they could afford to be thoroughly so. The shadow-and-line, thick as a felt-tip, interpreted Renaissance drawings. Like them of course, the colours were calm but not sombre – typically ochre, siena, umber; olive and sage green; shades of blue occasionally; and later in the century, Andreani with his varied areas of grey.

But if calm colouring from studio drawing is reflected in the prints, remarkable panache appears in its application. With rough Italian paper, the uneven inking of coloured areas could be used to create a background texture. Such a style of printing, which in book diagrams would merely strike us as inefficient, became a technique among the print-makers who managed to control it in imitation of water-colour drawing. One could call it the earliest form of aquatint.

Andrea Andreani of Mantua at the end of the century stretched the limits of this art and became something of a business man. Like other publishers he had the idea with so much existing and neglected work, of gathering it and issuing new editions; but being an artist he liked to work upon these blocks before re-issuing them. So we have a new life for the Italian chiaroscuro woodcuts, in second state and revised colouring according to Andreani's taste, with his monogram and date of publication. It would be interesting to trace their history as they passed through his control. His own magnum opus, ten prints after Mantegna illustrating the *Triumph of Caesar*, appeared in 1599 and have a place in Jackson's history; for the technique had been used till then to interpret drawing, and that series of paintings in Mantua offered a different challenge. Andreani was perhaps celebrating a centenary of his local artist's work. The existence of a set on purple silk, with gilding for the highlights, is evidence that his gesture carried a sense of occasion.

Though Jackson's route towards chiaroscuro was a strange one, we feel no surprise that he found his métier in Italy. Temperamentally, with distaste for 'the little exactness', he belonged there; but that was not his first technique, and as a young man he went across to Paris. England, it seems, had little to offer of a suitable sort in the early eighteenth century. A tradition of woodcut illustration continued in France.

Jackson travelled for work as an explorer, with ambitions. If France was the land, as ever, for art in illustration, it held no particular promise for his abilities. He had a formative but unsatisfactory time there. The chiaroscuro world, his resting place, had carried on fitfully since the high days of Andreani. Büsinck was the French practitioner in mid-seventeenth century, a German by origin. In the seventeen-twenties when Jackson came to Paris, Nicolas le Sueur and his brother Vincent were making a few prints of this sort – important because quite different from the wider world of woodcut and engraving, pioneers continuing the search for colour-printing; no longer quite alone, but in a small area of experiment.

Jackson, after conventional decorative cutting for Papillon, with whom he quarrelled, had the chance of sharing in a major work sponsored by Crozat, and undertaken by the Comte de Caylus, which would reproduce for publication some of the fine paintings and drawings held in French collections. Paintings by tradition were to be engraved, drawings would be done in chiaroscuro, and very considerable delicacy was achieved. Jackson may have had other ideas, but he is not the solo hero and provides no reason to denigrate the Cabinet de Crozat.

Many of those prints, not all, were made in the German manner, combining etched outline with woodcut background areas of light and shade. They strike me as able and sympathetic. Sometimes the etching would be done by Robert and chiaroscuro by Nicolas or Vincent le Sueur – the art was shared. Workshop woodcuts in Japan are not generally subject to criticism on that account. One may not accept the verdict of Jackson's biographer, that 'the combination method produced rather feeble prints that lacked the vigour of straight woodblock chiaroscuro'. Nicolas le Sueur performed with much delicacy, using quiet colours and highlight to mould his subject in depth. His form of originality perhaps lay in this accord with his models, a certain modesty. The style differed from earlier practitioners though he could manage, as in the *Diane et Endimion*, bold woodcut lines of the Italian school. The Cabinet de Crozat, viewed with work of its day, deserves attention and appreciation.

Jackson was about twenty-five when he went to Paris, thirty when he left. After the refusal by Crozat of a subject he had prepared in chiaroscuro, upon the advice of Caylus he set out for Rome. Illness delayed him in Marseilles, and he travelled instead by stages, job-hunting through Genoa and Florence towards Bologna and Venice. There he arrived in 1731, for a fourteen-year stay of mixed energy and modified rapture. His plans flew higher, but the best work by which we can recall him belongs to that Venice period.

For one thing, Zanetti was there – another kindred spirit with whom Jackson naturally quarrelled. These tensions from patrons stimulated him – Crozat in Paris, Zanetti in Venice. They were two patrons of the art to which his talent pointed. Others might offer more or less routine work, and he could perform it – fleurons, Bible cuts, the decorative border for a title page – but colour interpretation of drawings and paintings belonged with Crozat, or the *Raccolta di varie stampe a chiaroscuro*, woodcut prints after a collection of drawings by Mazzuola of Parma, Parmigianino, which had come into Zanetti's possession.

This Venetian count, born about 1680, collector and connoisseur, publisher and engraver, comes from the aesthetic world of eighteenth-century grand-tourism; accomplished, knowledgeable and possessive. Whether he used the knife on wood, or merely made the outlines and then engaged others to do so, may have seemed a smaller distinction to him than to Jackson. We may still hear someone say he has 'made' a rock garden or tennis court, when the sweat and work came from men he employed. Zanetti probably had what Walpole nicely called 'all the careful negligence of a gentleman'.

Anyway he lent one of the Parmigianino drawings – Venus and Cupid with a Bow – to Jackson, who copied it with such truth in the style of Ugo da Carpi that Zanetti added a few stains and wormholes to pass the result as antique; in the spirit of any garden architect whose new-built ruin caused general admiration. To our eyes that print falls some distance short of da Carpi, but the episode caused a parting of their ways in Venice.

Zanetti's prints, or the art he patronised, look pleasant enough and different now. If Ugo da Carpi was the influence, their style is more pastoral, arcadian. Where the areas of ochre and sepia are made with two blocks, with bold woodcut line and shadow, we have a new and successful style – not Jackson's or da Carpi's, but earning its place in the story – sometimes using shadow with minimal outline, often experimental. In the seventeen-twenties these represented an adventure, the Italian parallel with Crozat's enterprise but entirely from his own collection.

So we arrive at Jackson's Venice prints, but to understand their originality we must isolate that second quarter of the eighteenth century from later developments. Soft-ground etching had not appeared, aquatint was two decades away and lithography half a century. Ploos van Amstel, making every sort of experiment, issued his first prints in the late seventeen-fifties.

For the true theme of colour-printing, other than woodcut, we look back to another Dutchman, Joannes Teyler, in the last quarter of the seventeenth century. He inked one plate, à la poupée, varied his effects with some brilliance and was fascinated by colour. Teyler's prints, easily recognised, are rare. His plates, being engraved, give clear impressions. Colour was the equipment he played with – eight kinds together as delicate neighbours, never smudging or confused with each other; a paintbrush used perhaps for areas of sky and foreground.

Nobody followed Teyler, who was by temperament a miniaturist. Near his method but far from such effects, completely inking one plate, we have the charming and once-so-fashionable school of mezzotint colour prints, often using somewhat worn plates with harmonious results. Nearer to Teyler, needing more precision, were the colour-printed stipple engravings – by Bartolozzi for instance. But in the period of Jackson's Venice prints, Bartolozzi was still at Florence studying anatomy.

We can trace a more interesting eighteenth-century development back to the first edition of Newton's *Opticks*, 1704, directly related to Jackson because he felt defensive about it. Newton declared, as the editor puts it in his introduction to a modern edition of the *Opticks*, that 'ordinary white light is really a mixture of rays of every variety of colour'; adding that 'he seemed to be refuted by experiments in which a mixture of paints of two colours produced paint of a third colour and by other experiments belonging to the subjective physiological theory of colour-vision, in which colours really are compounded out of primaries'. Kainen refers to 'a simplification of Newton's seven primaries'. Nobody could suppose Newton was ignorant that yellow became green when mixed with blue, but his argument remained the ground of debate among printers experimenting with colour in the next half century. Newton's theory stimulated them, the norm from which each announced departure. Practice needed intellectual support, as Dürer used geometry to justify his taste in letter-forms; so we have a whole genre of print-makers' polemic and its modern application is colour television.

Jacob Christoph Le Blon, not to be confused with a man who imitated Baxter in the nineteenth century, lived from 1667 to 1741. Working from this 'simplification of Newton's seven primaries' he reproduced paintings by the use of mezzotint – not colouring the plate, as Teyler had, but mingling his red, blue and yellow by printing from three primary plates, each making its different contribution to colour and composition. Le Blon also used a black plate sometimes in his London period where people knew more about the *manière noire* than in Paris. His imitators, especially Jacques-Fabien Gautier Dagoty, claimed to have invented colour reproduction by adding the black plate; and though that caused something of a pamphlet war, it was nonsense. Le Blon, setting up as print-maker in London and Paris successively, failed on each occasion. Jacques-Fabien, briefly his pupil, mocked his memory by remarking how easy it was in England to win financial backing by the simple name-dropping device of basing one's theories upon Newton.

Le Blon's work is rare now, only about fifty prints recorded, and marvellous. It is particularly unusual to find it unsophisticated, because owners or dealers managed so to varnish and re-touch as to create a texture of fresh antiquity which could perfectly deceive quiescent guests in dark corners by candlelight. As colour separations of certain prints survive, there can be no controversy about Le Blon's technique.

Dates have some significance in this, for he died in 1741 and Gautier produced his first set of anatomy prints four years later – a moment which marks also the publication of Jackson's set of chiaroscuri in Venice. These large and extraordinary anatomy plates appeared from members of the Gautier Dagoty family – father and five sons – for the next thirty years, after which such new methods as aquatint pushed their labours aside. It remains an island of merit in art, science and printing.

But if we bear their dates in mind, it is evident that Le Blon loomed larger for Jackson. For the truth is Le Blon went a lot further by his reproductions of oil paintings, making in mezzotint gradations of colour which no subtlety could manage by woodcut with flat areas of plank. The rivalry existed, because Jackson too concerned himself with new colours which came from tint upon tint, writing in his Essay that 'Mr. Jackson has invented ten positive Tints in Chiaro Oscuro; whereas Hugo da Carpi knew but four; all which Tints can be taken off by four Impressions only.'

So Le Blon's achievement remained for him a background irritant. He wrote:

> It is not improbable that Gentlemen acquainted with Mr. Le Blond's Manner of Printing Engravings on Copper in colours, may imagine it to be the same with this of Mr. Jackson, and that from the former he has borrowed the Design; but whoever will take the least Pains to enquire into the Difference, will find it impossible, that the cutting on Wood Blocks, and printing the Impressions in various Colours from them, can be done in the same Way that is done with Copper Plates in the Metzotinto or Fumo Manner. Every Man who knows any Thing of the Nature of Engraving must be convinced, that those Metzotinto Plates, of all others, are the most liable to wear out; that it is impossible for any two Prints to be alike in their Colours when taken off in that Manner, and for this Reason, because the delicate and exquisite Finishings of the Flesh, and the tender Shadowings of all the Colours must be destroy'd; the very cleaning the Plates from one Colour to lay on another is sufficient to ruin all the fine Effect of the Workmanship, and render it impossible to take off ten Impressions without losing all the elegance of the Graving.
>
> On the contrary, this Method discovered by Mr. Jackson is in no Degree subject to the like Inconveniency; almost an infinite Number of Impressions may be taken off so exactly alike, that the severest Eye can scarcely perceive the least Difference amongst them.

Rather than accept a difference, and use it, the long life of wood compared with rocked and scraped copper struck Jackson as the point to stress.

As the Venice prints differed in kind from Le Blon's three-colour mezzotint, such rivalry appears now unnecessary; and Jackson's paragraph made a number of doubtful points. The shallow engraving of a mezzotint plate wore down, but colour on a worn plate had its own charm – in mezzotints by Ward after Morland, for example, so fashionable years ago; or in aquatint, the later issues of James Malton's Dublin. The distinction lay in method and effect, not merit

– they practised different forms of art, and were probably attempting different tasks.

Again, there is the debate about discovery and on this Jackson wrote a few specious sentences. Print-makers became jealous as to their claims of invention, much as the owners of private presses felt for the type faces they had designed (or commissioned, or copied). Le Blon pioneered three-colour printing, but nothing so irritated Gautier Dagoty as to be called the pupil of Le Blon – which, in every point of truth, he was.

Jackson showed a similar spirit, undisturbed by the long and delightful history of chiaroscuro since 1500. He wrote with disarming *naïveté* in the theme:

> At the same Time I am saying this in Favour of an Invention and inventor, it may perhaps be objected, that what this Person hath done, is not properly in Consequence of an Invention, since the same Art was known and put in execution by Albert Durer ... At Bologna also this Art received great encouragement, where the Works of Micharino di Siena, Andrea Andriano di Mantua, the Architecture of Serlio, and the Heads in Vassari's Lives of the Painters, were done in this Manner; and every great School in Italy adopted and cherished this Manner of Engraving and Printing.

What then? he continues:

> After having said all this, it may seem highly improper to give to Mr. Jackson the Merit of inventing this Art; but let me be permitted to say, that an Art recovered is little less than an Art invented. The Works of the former Artists remain indeed; but the manner in which they were done, is entirely lost: the inventing then the Manner is really due to this latter Undertaker, since no Writings, or other Remains, are to be found by which the Method of former Artists can be discover'd, or in what Manner they executed their Works; nor, in Truth, has the Italian Method since the Beginning of the 16th Century been attempted by any one except Mr. Jackson.

To us it reads oddly, off the point and inaccurate. Jackson never imitated anybody. As to interpretation and facsimile, it must always be a point of choice or temperament.

Morris objected that Hooper, cutting decorations on wood, following his 'theory of facsimile' would not interpret, remained loyal to his training of copying accurately. Every translator has to choose between literal reproduction and the style of his language. It is the old distinction between artist and camera – though the camera, like mezzotint, had a task of translating its coloured subject into black and white, or the artist's job of reducing from three dimensions.

One must reckon with printmakers that often by art rather than purpose the self came through. 'I have often dreamed of weeping,' Beatrice said in *Much Ado about Nothing*, 'but waked myself with laughter.' If Ugo da Carpi dreamed of copying, he must have waked himself with art. Chiaroscuro, always different and practised by few, was never a precision instrument; and Jackson was no exception, with his scorn for 'the little exactness'.

It is time to look at the Venice prints. Jackson writes:

> From a Conviction of the Truth of what has been said Mr. Frederick, Mr. Letheuillier, and Mr. Smith, the English Consul at Venice, encouraged Mr. Jackson to undertake to engrave in Chiaro Oscuro, Blocks after the most Capital Pictures of Titian, Tintoret, Giacomo Bassano, and Paul Veronese, which are to be found in Venice, and to this end procured him a Subscription.

Then he adds modestly,

> In this Work may be seen what engraving on Wood will effectuate, and how truly the Spirit and Genius of every one of those celebrated Masters are preserved in the Prints.

In reproducing paintings he carried his art to a new field. Except for Andreani's series after Mantegna, from 1599, chiaroscuro had not been used for the greater complexity of oil painting; but Jackson with his invention of 'ten positive Tints' advanced bravely. 'It is', he says, 'in this manner of doing Prints, as it is in the Works of the best Painters; the first Sketch of the design has very often an Elevation and Spirit of Expression, which is lost in the finish'd Picture.'

Trusting to Elevation and Spirit, fortified by ten Tints and Consul Smith's patronage, he sat with Titian's paintings through daylight in the Scuolo di San Rocco. One other element of innovation he used in the blocks for depth – embossing, inked or blind. If these prints are unpressed you cannot help running your finger over them, to feel the surface. Foliage in this way gained the detail of lace. A crop of errors accompanied, of course, such display of spirit and elevation. Printing damp upon damp, these large subjects creased as they dried; and if binders do their will, they press the life out. We must take Jackson buckled and embossed, with all faults and not subject to return; otherwise, as Enobarbus said of Cleopatra, 'you had missed a marvellous piece of work.'

Kainen called the Venice prints 'a daring effort to go beyond line engraving for reproducing paintings'. With Jackson's focus upon Spirit and Genius, we turn the leaves of one of the most extraordinary series of woodcuts ever issued; printed at his home in Venice upon the cylinder press constructed to his design, whose building nearly killed him; issued with its title page by Pasquali in 1745, the work of about five years; plates varying slightly in size but measuring roughly twenty-two inches by seventeen; most printed from four blocks; altogether ninety-four blocks, representing seventeen subjects on twenty-four sheets. Several can be joined as three or two, triptych or diptych, to form the complete picture.

The brilliance and daring of this work impress again each time one examines it. Perhaps we tend to see the embossing, to touch the chiaroscuro fold of drapery, muscles of a horse or wood grain; to wonder at the assurance of his sunrays, or the woodcut white of cloud form; to wish he had experienced such peace as his sleeping Disciples show on the Mount of Olives; to admire his stunning mastery of complexity in The Raising of Lazarus, after Leandro Bassano; foliage in The Entombment, after Jacopo Bassano; or to appreciate the experimental colours and embossed baroque decoration of two prints after Veronese: Holy Father and Four Saints, The Mystic Marriage of St. Catherine.

He, struggling in Venice, absorbed each painting and returned its spirit to us. Colour-harmonies, strength of impression and the lacework of embossing fascinate us technically, but this in 1740 was a responsible labour of translation. Rather than use, as he thought, shortlived mezzotint copper he followed an artist's way of interpreting. The forthright inks declare his character, and total absence of doubt in this choice of chiaroscuro.

We must admire, too, the restless work – overall texture of a master painting, nothing empty, few areas of wash or white. The whole became a study in varied density of form. And this, not his later work, brought to an end that road which went back to Ugo da Carpi. The thickness and bravura recall his genius, not the delicacy of Cranach or Hendrik Goltzius, and show his pleasure in fastidious detail of powerful labour.

In the general history of colour this is not the end; it is not the beginning of the end; but it may be the end of the beginning. This was the extreme of translated colour, a painting interpreted as tone and texture; overlapping, in Le Blon and Gautier Dagoty, a future of facsimile or literal colour.

Over this hill, or up it, Jackson strayed upon a slightly peculiar journey. Six immense prints in colours, after water-colour drawings by Ricci, followed the Pasquali publications and are seldom seen. The British Museum print room has them all, in various trial states. Such a voyage into colour reproduction has its historical place, as one source of the stream which would sweep up Savage, Baxter and Edmund Evans. Colours come into this group of woodcuts, as never before – patches of pink and red, bright blue, a whole mosaic. Something was preparing and Jackson had the vision to start it. Seventy years passed before anyone explored his example, and two more decades before it found proper practice. For those reasons, and rarity, one would like to have the Ricci prints. Peter Wick wrote at length about them, to Kainen they seemed his best achievement.

Jackson put the moment clearly in his *Essay*:

> Not content with having brought his Works in Chiaro Oscuro to such Perfection, he attempted to print Landscapes in all their original Colours; not only to give to the World all the Out-Line Light and Shade, which is to be found in the Paintings of the best Masters, but in a great Degree their very manner and Taste of Colouring.

So at last he was trying facsimile, his little exactness, with a lurch towards 'their very Manner and Taste of Colouring'; thereby pointing ahead, but marking the departure from his old art and betraying it. Colour is a concept musicians share; he was applying it now to the literal distinctions of red, blue, yellow and black. By attempting that form of truth, he lost illusion. As art his reds strike me like Cinderella's midnight.

Another use for them suggested itself, in his earlier plan to print woodblocks on wallpaper. Leaving Venice soon after the Pasquali publication he lived in Battersea, and the *Essay* from 1754 became a kind of rescue attempt for the wallpaper venture. Again, we may ignore his chronic claim as inventor: Papillon came of a wallpaper family, and so did Le Blon. Apart from painted hangings from China, this was the childhood of a thriving industry – but different from our concept of identical rolls which could fit in endless repetition.

'The papers in question consisted of various items', a contributor to the *Connoisseur* wrote fifty years ago, describing the manufacture in Jackson's day,

> centre, panels, borders, fillings, and so on, from which varying schemes of decoration could be arranged to suit the situation and the taste of the purchaser. The colouring was applied by hand by workpeople employed either by the manufacturer or by the patron. These were known as 'paper-stainers', and were of inferior position to the engraver, who ranked as something of an artist, though of the lower grades.

So Jackson cut pictures, or a simulation of sculpture, as prints in make-believe frames or for spaces within decorative borders. Such borders of fruit and frames exist in the British Museum collections – the Victoria and Albert Museum has a roll of his paper. As the purpose of his *Essay* was to sell wallpaper and offer examples a patron could choose, we may return to it for this late phase. He says

> To offer himself forth then to the Knowledge of his Country, is the
> Reason why the Author of that Paper-Manufactory now carrying on at
> Battersea, has printed these Sheets, in hopes that the illustrious Example
> above mentioned [patronage of the Duke of Cumberland] and the merit
> of the Undertaking, may induce Gentlemen of Taste to look into, and
> give Vigour to his Invention and Infant Art.

Kainen is a little contemptuous about the wallpaper enterprise,
but it deserves curiously just such honour as Morris received a century later when his energies turned in that direction. Like Morris he
despised the taste of his day, forthright about its absurdities. We shall
not find in Jackson's paper, for instance,

> Lions leaping from Bough to Bough like Cats, Houses in the Air, Clouds
> and Sky upon the Ground, a thorough Confusion of all the Elements,
> nor Men and Women, with every other Animal, turn'd Monsters, like the
> Figures in the Chinese paper, ever to be seen in this Work.

His scheme, opposite pole from Morris of course, was to have artificial alcoves for artificial sculpture, the gallery for a frustrated man
of taste:

> Thus the Person who cannot purchase the Statues themselves, may have
> these Prints in their Place; and may as effectually shew his Taste and
> Admiration of the ancient Artists in this manner of fitting up and finish-
> ing his Apartments, as in the most expensive.

Scaled down we have eight of Jackson's prints, a haphazard gathering, to make the Essay a kind of pattern book for wallpaper. Here are
Apollo and Democritus, a Lion against trees and rocks, a little clas-
sical temple called The Building and Vegetable; more statuary, a
pheasant, and garden ruin. For the pheasant and the ruin seven
blocks were used.

Nobody should legislate about taste, except the few who create it.
We can have nothing now to say about the dogma of either Morris or
Jackson. Flat woodblock areas of these prints could appear very sensibly, perhaps, as parts of a wall – naked upon its surface, not hang-
ing and framed. The technique fitted this absolute logic.

We lose sight of him after this Battersea failure, until Bewick's sad
recollection from much later, in the Memoirs:

> Jackson left Newcastle quite enfeebled with age, and, it was said, ended
> his days in an asylum, under the protecting care of Sir Gilbert Elliot,
> Bart., at some place on the border near the Teviot, or on Tweedside.

That was two decades still from the first lithography, but just after
Paul Sandby's aquatints of Wales, in the late seventies of the century
with which John Baptist Jackson passed his life.

6

Lord Chesterfield and his 'Characters'

Before viewing the strange history of Lord Chesterfield's *Characters*, those indiscreet portraits of public figures privately written, intended for oblivion and never fully published from that day to this, we should look again at Chesterfield who is commonly remembered or forgotten for letters to his son. He deserves another visit.

Publication of the letters of Philip Dormer Stanhope, fourth Earl of Chesterfield, was an aberration, which connects with current debate about what should be made known and what destroyed after death; for his world was no less fascinated by what they revealed about him, than ours by the printing of, say, letters from another Philip, the poet Larkin. The old Earl, famous for his wit and wealth, for philosophical calm and the reform of the calendar, for a period of liberal government in Ireland and valuable diplomacy at The Hague until deafness sent him into decades of retirement, was suddenly shown as providing a flow of advice to his unhappy son Philip on how to achieve useful liaisons with women and the crucial importance of false manners. Those two quarto volumes appearing in 1774, the year after Chesterfield died but six years after his son's death at the age of thirty-five – 'of a dropsy' in Provence it was said, but worn out perhaps by three decades of advice – have been read as an eighteenth-century model for success books, careers advice, how to succeed and influence people.

Defending Chesterfield is not the purpose of this essay, except to mention that he who had suffered from gaucherie and gracelessness and overcome them, who was short with a large head so that somebody in Hervey's hearing called him a stunted giant, wished to

defend Philip his son from similar miseries – especially when it
seemed that this awkwardness of manner was a heritage he had
bestowed. And Dame Catherine Cookson, a best-selling novelist
who reveres Chesterfield, wrote in her Introduction to short passages
from the letters:

> And you know, if I come across anyone who, when in conversation and
> Chesterfield's name is mentioned, says, 'Oh, Dr. Johnson said of him,
> "He had the manners of a dancing master and the morals of a whore"', I
> know instantly that the person has never read a serious word that Lord
> Chesterfield had written or that anyone else had written about him.

If Chesterfield is now remembered for what should never have
been published, that was just one aspect of illegitimacy which hacked
at the root of his difficult life. The mother of his son, Elizabeth du
Bouchet, was governess or companion to the Wassenaer family during his first spell as ambassador at The Hague. Quite unimaginable
in those days that Chesterfield should so ignore his station as to
marry her, but the notion of marriage came upon him perhaps as an
influence from the episode; for within a year he took to wife
Melusina von der Schulemburg, Countess of Walsingham, thirty-
nine years old and rich, illegitimate daughter of George the First's
mistress who had been created Duchess of Kendal. Chesterfield was
becoming a connoisseur of bastardy and this was an unusual form of
marriage. The countess continued to live with her mother, whom
Chesterfield described as little better than an idiot, while he established himself courteously in the house next door. That happy event
took place in 1733.

We leap across seventeen years to 1750 and Rome where his son
aged eighteen was enjoying a prolonged Grand Tour with a tutor
called Harte, author of a forgotten *Life* of King Gustavus Adolphus.
There Philip met the illegitimate daughter of an Irishman called
Domville, and no amount of sound advice or safe assumptions from
London and Bath prevented the kind of intimacy which Chesterfield
most dreaded. In Rome her father's family was not mentioned, she
went under the name of Eugenia Peters and though not especially
beautiful – by such accounts as remain – the rooms where she lived
with her mother, or companion (nobody knew, or knows), became
the haunt of certain English grand-tourists who could take a rest
from courtly manners to enjoy her playing on the harpsichord. No
doubt she had a pleasant Irish voice and, as most people from that
land, amusing conversation.

Lord Charlemont wrote his recollections of those youthful
months in Rome:

When I was at Rome together with my friend Lord Bruce, Stanhope and several other Englishmen, there arrived in that metropolis an elderly gentlewoman calling herself Mrs. Peters, with a young person, supposed to be her daughter, and named Miss Eugenia Peters. The difference between the mother and the daughter was obvious and striking even to our uninterested eyes. The former was a true English goody, vulgar and unbred; while the latter though plain almost to ugliness, had apparently received the most careful education, and was accordingly endowed with all the choicest accomplishments of her sex. She sang well, was perfect mistress of her harpsichord, and was in a word as elegant as her mother was vulgar. This unnatural contrast was however with us only the talk of an hour. As Englishwomen we frequented their lodgings, while some of the unoccupied among us, of which number Stanhope, in spite of his father's earnest and gallant exhortations, was one, persuaded themselves that they were smitten by the accomplishments of the amiable Eugenia. The ladies, having passed some months at Rome, set out for England, where, as I have been informed, the younger was owned by Mr. Domville, a well known and wealthy gentleman of Ireland, for his natural daughter.

Neither the unsuitable tutor nor distant supervision from his father having much influence over Philip's average behaviour in Rome, we may suppose they smiled together, Bruce and Charlemont and he, over the arrival of Chesterfield's letter written in January 1750, with its probe into affairs of the heart·

How go your pleasures at Rome? Are you in fashion there; that is, do you live with the people who are? ... Has any woman of fashion and good-breeding taken the trouble of abusing and laughing at you amicably to your face? Have you found a good *décrotteuse*? For these are the steps by which you must rise to politeness.

It was an unpleasant word to use, for *décrotteuse* means something which scrapes the mud off, or smooths down rough edges, but it so happened that he fell in love with his *décrotteuse*, remained loyal to the memory and married her.

Nobody can be sure whether Chesterfield knew about Eugenia's existence, or the marriage, before Philip's death made it necessary for him to learn both; it is most probable that he knew nothing until she acquainted him with several additions to his family: a widowed daughter-in-law and two grandsons, one already a teenager. Chesterfield was a great shock-absorber, his finest quality. He accepted Eugenia, much as he recognised Philip's mother, with one significant difference: though providing in his will for the two boys, to Eugenia he left nothing.

It is difficult now to imagine her predicament. Nobody knows when they married, but they had been acquainted for eighteen years.

Chesterfield showed no scruple in asking his friends to spy upon Philip, seeking reports of his conduct and bearing in Paris, Leipzig, Dresden, wherever he served and lived. In one place after another his son disappointed him, highest hopes of a philosopher-king descending at last to despair when an earnest prayer to his kinsman the Duke of Newcastle on Philip's behalf, for the residency at Venice when that place fell vacant, was rejected, making him 'too justly apprehend', as he wrote sadly, 'that Mr. Stanhope suffers chiefly from his relation to him who is with the utmost truth and respect, my Lord, Your Grace's etc.'

The truth dawned thus, in 1753; fifteen years of public failure for Philip followed, working against his temperament, enjoying under whatever conditions of strain and secrecy a kind of home. It is certain that Eugenia never accompanied him to the social events of a minor diplomat's life, or entertained in their house if they shared one; such news could not have been kept from the old Earl, and there is no hint of it in letters he wrote to Philip or any of his wide acquaintance.

How could she have thought of the tyrant and paymaster against whom rebellion was impossible, who had driven her marriage into disgrace and made family life secret? After her husband's death she needed the old man's help and to some extent received it, calling upon him at Blackheath, exchanging letters. It was a necessary connection to preserve, but she owed him absolutely nothing.

Eugenia was conscious of possessing, in addition to her sons and the memory of a husband, two hot literary properties – the extraordinary assembly of paternal letters preserved through Philip's boyhood, which he or she had continued to guard, and by chance that small group of free-ranging essays on Chesterfield's friends in high places, the *Characters*, sent at some time to Philip but never returned. Speculation may begin or end there, as to her motives for keeping them.

Dates now become of some interest. The old Earl died in March 1773. In September Gibbon declined an invitation to edit Chesterfield's letters to Philip – a month later Horace Walpole also declined. This risky responsibility fell then to the widow, in league with Dodsley as publisher from whom had come the impressive offer she could not refuse, fifteen hundred guineas. In November Dodsley drafted his 'Heads of Agreement', a document which rests in the Lilly Library at the University of Indiana. Here is the second of its two clauses:

> Mrs. Stanhope, in consideration of these conditions being duly performed by Mr. Dodsley doth engage to make over to him all her Rights

& Title to the Copy-Right of the said Earl of Chesterfield's Letters *and other Pieces*, to him & his Heirs forever.

[My italics]

There began an exciting chase between legal action and *fait accompli*, total deprivation and fifteen hundred guineas. It will be recalled that from her father-in-law's estate nothing was due to her. From legal risks and public scandal she had, literally, nothing to lose. In February 1774 trustees of the estate sought an injunction in the courts against publication, after Dodsley's announcement that two large quarto volumes of the letters would soon be available. As it affected those private and indiscreet essays, the *Characters*, this provides a very odd episode in the history of English publishing.

Here is the concise substance of Eugenia's defence, as printed in the English Reports:

> The Defendant, the widow, in her answer said, being frequently in company with Lord Chesterfield she one day mentioned to him, that she thought the letters he wrote to her late husband, would form a fine system of education if published, or to that effect; to which his Lordship answered, 'Why, that is true, but there is too much Latin in them', but did not express any disapprobation in publishing the same; and that some little time after such conversation, Lord Chesterfield requested her to restore to him some characters, which he had given to her late husband, declaring at the same time, upon his word and honour, that he desired to have those characters which were of particular people returned to him, only with an intent to burn or destroy them; and that she soon afterwards, about the latter end of the summer 1769, carried the characters to him, at his house at Blackheath, and at the same time took with her the letters, and that Lord Chesterfield took the original characters, and assured her upon his honour, that he meant to burn or destroy them, but declined taking the letters, or even looking at them, and told her she might keep them, or to that effect. She admitted that she has copies of the characters which she delivered to Lord Chesterfield, but the same are not nor ever were intended to be published in the books advertised to be sold, or any otherwise.

We have no reason to question the narrative truth of this passage, which provided an extraordinary confession.

I am not particularly concerned in this essay with the letters, though his reply in an exchange which sounds like badinage carries no weight; for Chesterfield wrote many letters to his son in French, but very few in Latin and they could well have been left out of the reckoning. More seriously he had recalled, with echoes from that idea of publication, the danger of casting into the world – *her* world, as she had proposed making a book – those pieces he had amused himself by writing, a few years earlier, about his friends and, alarming thought, the King and Queen.

In that paragraph reporting her statement in court, there are two significant time-intervals: 'some little time after such conversation, Lord Chesterfield requested her to restore to him some characters', that is the first. Not at once but 'soon afterwards, about the latter end of the summer 1769', she complied with his request, offering back both groups of manuscript, the letters and characters; yet Chesterfield accepted only the characters, declaring for the second time with emphasis, 'upon his honour', that he would burn them.

She may already have had a conversation with Dodsley, whose Heads of Agreement in 1773 referred to 'Letters and other Pieces'; either way her evidence was naïve. 'She admitted that she has copies of the characters ... but the same are not nor ever were intended to be published'. Can we be expected to believe that? Was Eugenia so fascinated by good prose and precious recollection, as to copy those essays which upon his word and honour the Earl intended to destroy?

Her case rested, and a couple of legal arguments followed, straightforward on the part of the trustees but specious on hers in a style familiar to this day. On behalf of the plaintiffs it was urged:

> That Lord Chesterfield taking the characters and leaving the letters in her hands, is not evidence of his consent to her printing the letters. He did not choose that the characters should be shewn to any body, nor seen even by chance, and therefore burnt them ... That the widow appears to have misbehaved in keeping copies of the characters; and though she says they were not intended to be published in the books advertised, or any otherwise, yet she may alter her mind, and do it some time or other, unless restrained by injunction.

On her side it was argued:

> That the letters contain a system of education, and instructions, and would be serviceable to the public. That Lord Chesterfield, if living, would have no objection to their being printed, and in fact did make no objection, when the widow mentioned to him in conversation, that they would form a fine system of education if published, but said there was too much Latin in them. That when Lord Chesterfield declined taking the letters, and told her she might keep them, he meant she might do as she pleased with them ...

Dodsley and Eugenia had of course known very well what they were doing and chose to risk it, perhaps from some other motive than service to the public.

The case rested, Lord Apsley deliberated. His judgment like the pleading was entirely able, in good traditions of English law, mixing its strict application with a twist of common sense. As to the strict application, he

> was very clear that an injunction ought to be granted. That the widow had no right to print the letters without the consent of Lord Chesterfield, or his executors. That she had obtained neither the one nor the other. That Lord Chesterfield, when he declined taking the letters, and said she might keep them, did not mean to give her leave to print and publish them. That she did very ill in keeping copies of the characters, when Lord Chesterfield meant that they should be destroyed and forgot.

He agreed the executors should have applied earlier for their injunction, 'before the expence of printing was incurred', and concluded by quoting four comparable cases where injunctions had been granted against publication of letters – including that of Pope against Curll.

It must all have sounded very depressing as Eugenia watched her guineas sink below the horizon. Then a surprising conclusion to this case, the twist of common sense giving hope that all was not lost:

> Ordered an injunction till hearing, but recommended it to the executors to permit the publication, in case they saw no objection to the work upon reading it, and having the copies delivered to them.

So it was up to the trustees, and the others faced a few anxious days; then it was all over and these two trustees, Beaumont Hotham and Lovell Stanhope, free of vindictiveness, signed their statement in accord with Lord Apsley's suggestion; as the letters were already in print and copies had reached Ireland beyond recall, and having read the book there seemed nothing absolutely offensive, publication could proceed. But they introduced one condition: Chesterfield having destroyed his manuscripts of the *Characters* (so they had understood in court, but their advisers might have been more thorough in checking the point), they insisted before publication of the letters went ahead that Eugenia's copy-manuscript of the *Characters* be burnt in their presence. Here is the text of that statement which survives at the Lilly Library, in the hand of Beaumont Hotham:

> To Mrs. Eugenia Stanhope, and Mr. James Dodsley
> London March 29 1774

> We have perused the printed copy of Lord Chesterfield's letters, and tho there are some things in them which it might have been better to have omitted, yet in consideration of the Copy being actually printed off, an Edition coming out in Ireland, and above all the Chancellor's Recommendation to the Executors to permit the publication, if there was nothing very improper contained in it, as also of Mrs. Stanhope's

having this day assured us under her hand, that she has not taken nor suffered to be taken any Copy of certain manuscript Characters, which are lodged with her Counsel Mr. Dunning, for the purpose of being burnt in our presence, as soon as he shall return to London, and that she has no other letters of the late Earl, excepting some private letters to herself, which she never intended, nor does not intend to publish, but which she desires to retain as Tokens of his Lordship's Affection for her, we now waive the Injunction that has been obtained against her and Mr. Dodsley, and do Consent to the publication of the said work, according to the Copy transmitted to us.

      Beaumont Hotham   Ll Stanhope

The great gamble of rushing into print had succeeded. Eugenia had no scruple about burning the *Characters* for her fifteen hundred guineas; Dodsley was happy to ignore those 'other pieces' in the heady prospect of bringing out his books at a moment when the court case had increased public expectation. The two trustees had acted rather hastily, and 'perused' the quarto volumes at record speed.

That, it seemed, concluded the life of Chesterfield's *Characters*. The lawyer for the trustees had believed so, saying clearly that Chesterfield 'did not choose that the characters should be shewn to any body, nor seen even by chance, and therefore burnt them'. Now there was a second fire, in Mr. Dunning's presence, to destroy Eugenia's manuscript of them and she assured the two trustees 'under her hand that she has not taken nor suffered to be taken any Copy ...' This news spread fast and inaccurately, Walpole writing to Mason nine days later about the case:

> At last his Lordship permitted the publication on two conditions, that I own were reasonable, though I am sorry for them. The first, that the family might expunge what passages they pleased: the second that Mrs. Stanhope should give up to them, without reserving a copy, Lord Chesterfield's Portraits of his contemporaries, which he had lent to his son, and re-demanded of the widow, who gave them up, but had copied them. He burnt the originals himself, just before he died ...

Well, the truth was a little different: Eugenia watched as the copy she had made burnt to ash in Mr. Dunning's presence; Chesterfield, despite those declarations upon his word and honour, did not destroy his manuscript of the *Characters*. They survive. Passages in them suggest he was writing for posterity rather than the flames but an air of polished irresponsibility, relaxing to him as delightful for us, demanded a pause before full public exposure. It is a brief work. There was really no need for it to wait two hundred and thirty years.

The history of these character-sketches, as they leaked into print, is quickly told. Seven appeared in a small book 'Printed for William Flexney, Holborn 1777': *Characters of Eminent Personages of His Own Time, Written by the late Earl of Chesterfield; and Never Before Published*. Nobody knows how Flexney, an obscure bookseller, got hold of them but Edward and Charles Dilly, of more substance, who had brought out two stout volumes of Chesterfield's *Miscellaneous Works* in that same year, hastened to produce a slender quarto uniform with those, *Characters by Lord Chesterfield Contrasted with Characters of the Same Great Personages by other respectable Writers ... Intended as an Appendix to His Lordship's Miscellaneous Works*. That came in 1778, separately issued, but sheets of it were bound into their next quarto edition of the *Miscellaneous Works* and are generally seen thus. The Dilly edition has sixteen characters – drastically censored of course, and adding passages of praise from other authors to fend off possible trouble in the courts.

And there the *Characters* rested, until Lord Mahon's octavo edition of the *Letters* in five volumes, 1845 and 1852. In the second volume Mahon, a member of the Stanhope family with access to family papers, arranged or re-arranged them as twenty essays, including a political account of Bute's Administration which does not belong there. Asterisks in Mahon's edition (reprinted by Henry Bradshaw in the 1890s) do not indicate the extent of his omissions. Most gaps occur in an admirably free-ranging essay, longest of them all, on the Mistresses of George the Second. Mahon chopped and divided that, asterisked and titled it.

It is time to quote, and illustrate, for apart from the royal family he was writing about Pope, Arbuthnot, Bolingbroke, Walpole, Scarborough, Newcastle, Pitt, Pulteney: a worthwhile assembly. Chesterfield deaf but at peace in his house at Blackheath, called now The Ranger's House and well looked after by English Heritage, scribbled what he pleased of an evening, drafted and revised. Two versions of his essays on Pitt and on Bolingbroke, for example, survive among the manuscripts in his hand. Though the extent of changes cannot now be discovered, we should receive the *Characters* as re-written spontaneity. There are phrases in his piece on Pope which seem appropriate to them: 'I have been with him a week at a time at his house at Twickenham', he tells us, 'where I necessarily saw his mind in its undress, when he was both an agreeable and instructive companion'. The merit of his *Characters* is that we see their author's mind in its undress as an instructive and agreeable companion. There is space for half-a-dozen brief passages, in no particular order.

Of Newcastle, a kinsman under whose administration Chesterfield achieved the reform of the Calendar:

His ruling, or rather his only passion was the agitation, the bustle, and the hurry of business, to which he had been accustomed above forty years, but he was as dilatory in dispatching it, as he was eager to engage in it. He was always in a hurry, never walked but always run, insomuch that I have sometimes told him, that by his fleetness one should rather take him for the Courier, than the Author of his own letters.

Of Arbuthnot and his brave death:

He lived and dyed a sincere and devout Christian. Pope and I were with him the Evening before he dyed, when he suffered racking pains from an inflammation in his bowels, but his head was clear to the last. He took leave of us with tenderness without weakness, and told us that he dyed not only with the comfort, but even the devout assurance of a Christian.

By all those who were not much acquainted with him, he was considered infinitely below his level; He put no price upon himself, and consequently went at an under value; For the world is complaisant or dupe enough, to give every man the price he sets upon himself, provided it be not insolently and overbearingly demanded. It turns upon the manner of asking.

On Pope and his view of Christianity:

Pope in conversation, was below himself, he was seldom easy and natural, and seemed afraid that the man should degrade the Poet, which made him always attempt wit and humour, often unsuccessfully, and too often unseasonably ... Having mentioned his being a Deist, I cannot forbear relating a singular Anecdote not quite foreign from the purpose. I went to him one morning at Twickenham and found a large folio Bible with gilt clasps, lying before him upon his table, and as I knew his way of thinking upon that book, I asked him Jocosely, if he was going to write an answer to it. It is a present said he or rather a legacy from my old friend the Bishop of Rochester. I went to take my leave from him yesterday in the Tower, where I saw this Bible upon his table. After the first compliments, the Bishop said to me, my friend Pope, considering your infirmitys, and my Age and exile, it is not likely that we should ever meet again, and therefore I give you this legacy to remember me by. Take it home with you and let me advise you to abide by it. Does your Lordship abide by it your self? – I do, – If you do My Lord it is but lately. May I beg to know what new light, or arguments, have prevailed with you now, to entertain an opinion so contrary to that which you entertained of that book, all the former part of your life? The Bishop replied, we have not time to talk of these things, but take home the book, I will abide by it, and I recommend to you to do so too, and so god bless you.

Of the Queen:

Queen Caroline had lively pretty parts, a quick conception, and some degree of Female Knowledge, and would have been an agreable woman in social, if she had not aimed at being a great one in Publick life. She had the graces that adorn the former, but neither the strength of parts, nor the Judgement necessary for the latter. She professed Art, instead of concealing it, and valued herself upon her skill in simulation and dissimulation, by which she made herself many enemys, and not one friend, even among the women the nearest to her Person. She loved money, but could occasionally part with it, especially to men of learning, whose Patronage she affected. She often conversed with them, and bewildered herself in their Metaphysical disputes, which neither she, nor they themselves understood.

Of King George the Second:

As Elector of Hannover, he thought himself great, as King of great Brittain only rich. Avarice, the meanest of all passions was his ruling one, and I never knew him deviate into any one generous action. Little things, as he has often told me himself, affected him more than great ones, and this was so true that I have often seen him put so much out of humour at his private Lévée, by a mistake or blunder of a Valet de Chambre, that the gaping Crowd admitted to his Publick Lévée, have, from his looks and Silence concluded that he had Just received some dreadfull news. Tacitus would always have been deceived by him.

And here is the final paragraph of his essay, most of it unpublished until now, on the Mistresses of George the Second:

In the mean time the Queen was greatly puzzled what to do. Lady Suffolk's place she was sensible must and would be filled up, and knew that it was the only Post in the Kingdom of which she had not the absolute disposal. The King's taste was to be considered a little, but not be flattered too much, so that for the interim she laid Lady Deloraine in his way, who with a beautyfull face, had the silliest head, and the most vicious heart that ever were created. The King took a taste of her, but did not like that taste well enough to take any more of that piece. He was now exceedingly upon his own hands, and fluttered about seeking where he could find rest. When Miss Mordaunt one of the Queen's Maids of honour seemed to fix him. She had an assemblage of beautyfull features with a fine complexion. But she had the Breasts of an overgrown wet Nurse, and the voice of a Boatswain. Her Arms were small and square, and ridiculously disproportioned to so prominent a Chest. She was egregiously Silly, but as good as she was silly. A warm benevolence of heart made her love every body, and perhaps hindered her from being in Love with any body. The King distinguished her Publickly by attentions very unusual in him, and the Queen seemed upon the whole to approve of his

Choice, trusting to the imbecillity of the Lady. But now comes the surprising part of the Story. The King to my certain knowledge offered her
Titles, and great settlements, which I am sure he had never done before
nor since to any woman living. All in vain; She proved a Maid of honour
in the litteral sense, and not in the usuall acceptation of that word. She
would not listen even to a King, reminded by her Catechism which I
dare say she repeated every day, that she had at her baptism renounced
all the pomp and vanity of this wicked world and all the Sinfull lusts of
the flesh. She afterwards Married Mr. Poyntz a very worthy man with a
very Small fortune.

It would be just to end by recalling the character of Lord
Chesterfield in two or three of his minor aphorisms which have nothing to do with a dancing master's manners or a whore's morals,
showing rather the recluse of Blackheath who had found a peaceful
exit from many private problems.

Perhaps his failure as patron of Johnson's *Dictionary* was due to
neglect of his own advice offered later, in 1765, to the boy who
would inherit the title as fifth Earl. Nine years old, he was told in a
letter that

> the great, the rich, and the powerfull, too often bestow their favours
> upon their inferiors, in the manner, that they bestow their scraps upon
> their dogs, so as neither to oblige man or dog. Let us then not only scat-
> ter benefits, but even strew flowers for our fellow travellers, in the rugged
> ways of this wretched world.

He knew the dangers of wit, had caused enough harm with that
weapon, and declared it was as important for a man to live within his
wit as within his income. If God give you wit, he told the same boy,

> which I am not sure that I wish you, unless he gives you at the same time
> an equall portion of Judgement to keep it in good order, wear it like your
> Sword in the scabbard, and do not brandish it to the terror of the whole
> company. If you have real wit it will flow spontaneously and you need
> not aim at it, for in that case the rule of the Gospel is reversed, and it will
> prove, seek and you shall *not* find. Wit is so shining a quality, that every
> body admires it, most people aim at it, all people fear it, and few love it
> unless in themselves.

Of less certain morality but to me wholly sympathetic is advice to
his son in 1749, for one must not ignore Chesterfield as stylist:

> An unharmonious and rugged period, at this time, shocks my ears; and
> I, like all the rest of the world, will willingly exchange and give up some
> degree of rough sense, for a good degree of pleasing sound.

Irreproachable as commonplace to the general, but full of doubt to me, was his forthright dogma written in that same year to Philip who showed worrying signs of becoming a book-collector: 'Due attention to the inside of books, and due contempt for the outside, is the proper relation between a man of sense and his books'.

7

The Prison Manuscripts of Ackermann's Hack

William Combe is best remembered as poet of Doctor Syntax. Collections of his papers exist where one would expect to find them but most of the work he did for Ackermann, and to provide text for Rowlandson's aquatint illustrations, is in two folio volumes which Professor Harlan Hamilton calls the Fleming Papers. These have now come back to England from New York and are the subject of this essay.[1]

The last quarter-century of Combe's life was spent in King's Bench prison as a busy scribbling debtor, and during it he made the reputation which lives. Before, he had written satirical or political books and became editor of *The Times*; after, he was associated with the most enterprising publisher in the visual history of books. As Professor Hamilton says in his biography,

> For the rest of his life Combe was to be engaged in this kind of journeyman work, writing prose and verse to accompany aquatints, chiefly those turned out by Ackermann's staff or engravers and colourists. The books produced by this collaboration include many items highly prized by collectors today: *History of Westminster Abbey* (1812), *Antiquities of York* (1813), *Poetical Sketches of Scarborough* (1813), the histories of *Oxford* (1814), *Cambridge* (1815), the *Colleges* (1816), *Madeira* (1821), and most important of all his work with Rowlandson, the three *Tours of Doctor Syntax* (1812, 1820, 1821), the *Dance of Death* (1815, 1816), the *Dance of Life* (1817), and *Johnny Quae Genus* (1822). During these

---

[1] I bought them at John Flemming's shop, in the astonishing days – not so long ago – when such treasure could exist and wait unregarded from one visit to the next.

years he also produced similar books for other publishers, including *The Thames, or Graphic Illustrations* (1811), *Picturesque Views on the Southern Coast* (1826), and *Pompeii* (1827).

The two folio volumes, with manuscript of almost all the books in Professor Hamilton's paragraph, belong to his prison years. These are the pages covered in confinement, as he lived in discipline, working and earning; but the sacramental character of such a manuscript rests in the presence there of the man himself. Here is old Combe, doggerel to the left of a sheet and rough accounts in space on the right – 'Mrs R, £13 —, Hair – 6', and (a large bill) 'Butcher 4–17–10 ½'; or beyond his verse frontier come draft petitions to the Prince, blurbs for Ackermann, letters to his friend Maria Brooks. Some are out of order, upside-down, or verses over the faded ink of his history of an Oxford college.

An early note, from bookseller or auctioneer no doubt, is bound into the beginning:

> Combe's (Dr) Manuscripts in one thick folio volume containing the originals of Dr. Syntax, Quae Genus, Accounts of Public Edifices & Schools, the University of Oxford, various Histories of Towns, Essays, Poems, Works written for professed Authors who could not write themselves, a curious defence written in the name of Marshal of the King's Bench concerning his Conduct in connection with Lord Cochrane's escape & giving several curious particulars of the circumstances attending the same, and many other things altogether a very interesting volume but in sad confusion having been very badly used by the Doctor himself who wrote just where the book opened, either end upwards very imperfect – many places the original manuscript has been covered by a second composition being written over it with a coarse pen.

This eloquent paragraph suggests the charm of Combe's manuscript, and quality of his life ('either end upwards very imperfect'). Though their early history is unknown, a letter from his bigamous and estranged wife Charlotte to Ackermann, soon after Combe's death, records the existence of manuscripts which may well be these. Unhappily she cannot manage to pay his

> debts unless the M.S. Papers which you kindly Collected and which are in Mrs Ryves's hands should prove deserving your acceptance. – Anthony mentions that you thought some were of value. I have the smallest Idea what they contain, and therefore you are the best judge if they are worth more than the £90 – due to Mrs R – I can only say that I should be most happy could I present them to you *unincombered* by so havey a Debt –

As they are his chief work from the prison decades, it seems unlikely any other later gathering of Combe's manuscripts would then have been reckoned 'of value'. In the author's hand a preliminary page is headed 'K. Acquaintance with Ackermann 1809'. Combe in his writing used K to stand for King's Bench. It seems they came to Ackermann in one folio volume but late in the nineteenth century somebody bound the collection handsomely in two, contriving to gild the edges without damaging text.

One fascination of Combe's chaos was his pursuit of literary success in the King's Bench prison, and preservation of self-respect. As a hack his position appears in some pride of definition. 'For my ordinary drudgery', he tells one correspondent for whom he has worked, 'I shall be paid my ordinary price'. Upside down in the middle of an account of Switzerland, upon the top of other matters, appears an uncompleted thought,

> But whatsoe'er may be the station
> Where chance may find my next vocation –

This was his station – hack, professional writer, freelance. On the right of *Quae Genus* verses he gives out of the blue a list of work he can recall over the years, including

> Not less than 2,000 columns in Newspapers. – The minor contributions I do not presume to number – memoranda of 64 memorials to different boards, &c. for various Applicants – 73 Manuscript Sermons, some of which were published –

Then he wanders to the Ackermann years of steadier work and a prison home:

> Various Assistances in verse in his poetical Magazine; as illustrations of its plates. For several years a monthly Contributor to Ackermann's literary repository – The Female Tatler, through several years of monthly continuation; but in them I had frequent assistant contribution.

The manuscripts show how Ackermann called upon his help for the minor chores which now belong to a publicity staff. The painting and construction of carriages interested Ackermann all his days, so when a book on the theme is ready Combe provides its advertisement. The ingenious publisher had invented and patented a kind of movable axle. 'The Utility derivable from building carriages with these Axles' he has to grind out, 'or adding them to old ones it is confidently presumed will be proved to the satisfaction of every one who will favour this work partial attention'. A subscription list is needed for a proposed publication, following the success of his *Oxford* and *Cambridge* – a *History of the Colleges*, the work now known as

'Ackermann's Public Schools'; so Combe drafts a form of appeal to the public. A prefatory note for the *Third Tour of Doctor Syntax* is scribbled, and a blurb for the newly completed *Dance of Life*. Princess Charlotte has died, Ackermann issues prints of her; subscriptions are invited, so Combe prepares the notice. He gives also an example of poems to be provided with them – 'illustrations of its plates', in his own humble phrase. As poet this lay some way from his line of country:

> O much lov'd Princess, o'er thy dear remains
> Music laments in unavailing strains
> Through Death's long night. Faith sheds her cheering ray
> And lights the passage to eternal day.

Though writing to order can never have been simple as it seems, Combe in old age came near the end of invention and we find him drafting a letter to a lady, when the *Dance of Life* was on, at a loss for situation or episode to illustrate Rowlandson:

> I am rather flattered that you should think the Dance of Death to be a superior production in point of Composition to Dr. Syntax: – because that opinion is my own; – & it has occurred to me to form a work as a companion to it, to be named the Dance of Life. Now, most excellent Lady, will you either beneath a Laurel or at your own table, or in your dressing Room, will you beckon a Muse to come to you – There are seasons when the Plough-share is still; when the activity of vegetation is silent, & Labour enjoying the comparative Indolence of Expectation. You might then vary, or rather occupy the Scene, by calling into activity the extraordinary powers you possess in the way which I propose – If they were only your first thoughts I would thank you for them (In any verse, in any measure) – The secret is now out: – I shall say no more (on the subject).

The old bookseller's description of the manuscript is pleasantly true of some parts. Passages of *Quae Genus* come over the top of Combe's account of Merton College for Ackermann.

> And in the scramble on the table
> He got as much as he was able

we learn, reading between the lines. Notes about Queen's College appear on the back of a cutting about racing at Newmarket, from the *Sporting Intelligence* of 1808 – so helping to date the early pages of these volumes. They live as a study of method, Combe's working day.

Other aspects of Ackermann's enterprise also needed Combe's help. Though we remember him for aquatint, he was early in England to use lithography – a friend of Senefelder its inventor, issuing examples of the new method in his *Repository of the Arts* and bringing out the English version of Senefelder's book in 1818. The public had to be aware of such development. A tax on lithographic stone was proposed, and Combe drafts with some labour and correction a rather specious argument against it. His draft is literally transcribed:

> A motion having been made in Parliament to introduce a Bill for the purpose of imposing a Duty on Calcareous Stones employed in the Art of Lithography now introduced into this Country, and which promises a new feature in the Arts hitherto unknown or which has not been practised in GB I beg leave to submit to your consideration such reasons as my extensive experience suggests me on a subject in which the fine Arts and a very considerable branch of trade are materially interested. Lithography, though well known, as it is most extensively to the very great Advantage of the places where it has been more particularly cultivated and encouraged – It is however but new in this country, though if cultivated and encouraged promises uncommon improvement in a branch of the fine Arts, which have taken such a deep root in the British Soil, and form such beneficial article in the trade of it.
>
> It is a commercial principle founded in a just sense of public Interest & political Justice, that new Inventions should ever be nourished and protected: – in order to raise them into that Importance, Stability and general adoption which may allow for their extensive circulation of being subject to future Taxation. – The Species of Stone which is proposed to be Taxed is to be found in England but by no means of a quality sufficient to allow of execution equal to that brought from Germany, and the latter is brought 1000 miles, from the interior of that Country, and so great an expense, that any Tax made payable thereon would amount to a Prohibition. – Besides the Quantity imported would be comparatively so small, that it could not be worth the attention of Government to impose it. Indeed it would appear to be a wiser rather to propose a bounty to encourage their –

Two pages later he prepares a letter, to the Society of Arts, which will go with a copy of Senefelder's book and canvass its suitability for a reward the Society has offered 'for the improvement of this among other important discoveries'. Publicity on behalf of new discovery could not have come easily to Combe in his eightieth year; but he could generally call upon Ackermann for money, and the charge was reversed for these occasional chores.

As comic poet, Combe's position remains a strange one and his method unaccountable. For years he never spoke with Rowlandson, but in some partnership of temperament invented his long verse episodes as text for the drawings which arrived. From accident, it seems to have become a condition of work. To advertise the *Dance of*

Life he drafts a note, explaining that if 'a more intimate connection has taken place between the Artist and the writer, the same principle has in a great measure if not altogether predominated in the structure of this composition, as in that of the Tour of Dr. Syntax & the Dance of Death'.

Though it would be foolish to examine the manuscripts in thesis-detail for working method, ample evidence is there. He seems to have written fluently, almost in a coma once the flow started. There are changes, afterthoughts and deletions of course, but in thousands of lines relatively few. An oddity of the *Second Tour of Doctor Syntax* is the tiresome length of obituary at the start, for his stupid wife Dolly who had been an entertaining figure of ridicule while she lived. It is therefore of some interest to observe that Combe wrote these passages emotionally, with more care and correction than most of his verse received, some passages transposed, new ink and handwriting as of a long session ended and a fresh start when she is truly dead.

One follows the progress of his Madeira book through that Regency mixture of third-hand history and foolish doggerel at the service of entirely charming art. The faithful and famous account of a Skimmington ride, as Syntax observes the procession of Yorkshire villagers teasing the life out of a man who lets himself be too much bullied by his wife, is here – and the touching visit of Syntax to Nimrod, old Apperley the sporting writer, for which Combe makes notes of a few likely dog names before using them in his verse lines.

And there is the pleasure of finding first drafts of successful passages from several of the books – as for instance the embarrassment of Sir Henry in the *Dance of Life*, when he confesses financial trouble which rules out the new barouche on which his wife had set her hopes. This differs slightly from the published version:

> As for Barouches, be it known
> I soon, dear girl, may sell my own.
> There's a sad rent in my affairs,
> But you I know will sooth my cares!
> Though the world frowns you will beguile
> My downcast spirits with a smile,
> Now till this cloud is past and over
> We both must cease to live in clover
> In humble style you'll be content, –
> Besides you have your settlement
> When redd'ning up she fiercely said,
> And *I know too, if 'tis not paid*
> *That you in Limbo* shall be laid,

> The contest warmd and words arose
> Which I shall leave to vulgar prose,
> My Muse is chaste nor would rehearse
> The criminating slang in verse.
> But she will tell with vixen grace,
> Miss threw the coffee in his face,
> And in her passion's wild Uproar
> Dash'd all the Crock'ry on the floor,
> And spurn'd him, in the way of trade,
> From out the House for which He paid.

It would be absurd to search Combe's on-demand writing for news about his private life, though the deep irony in the characterization of Vellum, the bookseller, comes undisguised from memory. In such a scattering of notes and drafts from a working life spent in King's Bench prison, hints and points of view abound.

The years never diminished his pleasure in mild intrigue or playful exchange with women. He must have been in correspondence, as we know he was at dinner parties, a charming but unscrupulous friend. Here in old age is his Valentine to Miss S— W—:

> While I behold her animated Face
> Her gentle goodness and her native grace
> Her early mind each well-trac'd charm receives
> From the example which a mother gives.
> Take then the praise sincere for such is mine.
> Thus sings her faithful, grey-hair'd Valentine.
> And shall I now awake the untuneful String
> Strain my weak voice and in my winter sing
> But you inspire and will accept the Lays
> That fond Affection to her virtue pays.

This was unexceptionable, but Combe's life had more puzzling troubles. After the insanity of his first wife he tended to ignore the wretched connection and married Richard Cosway's sister-in-law Charlotte. When that failed and she crossed to Ireland he formed friendships of inconstant strength and seriousness of purpose. The manuscripts are scattered with ample evidence in letters, verse or long complaint. One of his last and strangest books, the collection of letters to Maria Brooks, took its course over this period and near the end he asks for their return, having publication in mind. One long draft letter, an apology and explanation for eloping, must have been written (like so much of his work) to solve the distress of another life. Combe became a kind of third-party insurance premium.

It is therefore the more moving when a different voice speaks and one hears him for a moment, for we have listened to chatter and missed the man. After harsh words about a poem submitted for his criticism, he goes on (transcribed literally):

> And now for your important Questions. – I am not happy for I am a human being to whom happiness is not a natural & therefore not a possible possession: but I am perfectly content, and therefor so happy as I can, or ought to be. – Death never was an object of terror, in the gaieties, pleasures and splendor and sad meridian of Life. Nor am I now, when I am now when in two months I shall attained 76 Years, and am in the near neighbourhood of his Domain. – I never could think death an Evil, because it is universal; and an universal evil, cannot be the work of all good, just & merciful Being, who made us subject to it. – Life has ever appeared to me as a probationary State, I cannot reconcile it to reason under any other character, a future being must follow it – Besides, the belief of another Life, is a belief as universal as Life itself: – and he who made man would not have inspired with this Idea, wherever he lives & breathes, if it had not been among the Decrees of Heaven:– Besides, I have an internal conviction, an inexplicable conscience, superior to all reason, from the contemplation of my own frame & the powers that direct & govern, that I have an immortal spirit within me. Our nature is combination of the Brute and the Angel. – when the former perishes, the latter gains its freedom & is itself again.

Artistic judgment appears in these drafts of letters and articles – upon Lord Byron for instance, and the Royal Academy about which he is amusingly satirical:

> It still continues to be, in a predominant measure, a collection of portraits, and a Stranger might be led to suppose from a view of it, that the English people preferred as pictures the faces of their Friends or their own to any other subjects.

He admires 'Sir James Lawrence' and praises Turner in so far as he imitated Claude Lorrain, but cannot digest his unorthodox treatment of a sky, 'the sole defect in this magnificent Landscape'. As for architecture, a few notes towards an essay express impeccable principles: 'There are those who mistake whim for Genius and ornament for taste. Use is the first object, & then beauty follows'.

So he lived, using a moderately comfortable room in the 'State House', the privileged part of the prison, as his working study; dining out with Walter of *The Times* or with Ackermann's family, visiting the Academy and taking long country walks. Debtor's prison, for such as him or Leigh Hunt, seems to have been viewed with absolute tolerance in social courtesy. At Combe's time of life the place may have looked to him and others as we perhaps see an Old People's Home, and he as a guest suffered no more embarrassment than a visitor now from any comparable institution. His own view of King's Bench confirms this, and appears clearly more than once. He had worked it out, or accepted it, and one must be impressed by the sensitivity of the time which digested such an attitude towards debt and among debtors.

Their creditors may have felt otherwise, but anger was pointless and the prison notion came nearer to therapy than revenge:

> Imprisonment is not to be considered as a state of Punishment, but as a provisional Security of the Debtors person, of which the Creditor has thought proper to take possession, till the debt is paid or such other compensation is made, as shall satisfy the Creditor. And if it appears that such security is amply guaranteed by the Rules as by the enclosures, it does not appear that the C[reditor] sustains any injury, by their being allowed to remain, as they have been immemorially established.

> One of the great distresses and injurious results to debtors, who have a prospect of settling with their Creditors, or a wish by personal Exertions and oeconomical Habits to attain that object, is a separation from their families, which is prevented by the means which the R[ules] afford of preventing such a disunion ...

> Why are not debtors who are among the superior ranks of Life, for such there are, to be allowed indulgences suited to their habits of their situation & education, provided those Indulgences do not lessen the security which the Cr. claims from the walls of a Prison ...

Long passages of the manuscripts describe and defend the reasonable living conditions of imprisoned debtors. As there is no room to quote these at length, one may simply note their agreeable cause; for it seems the Marshall of the King's Bench needed to defend himself against serious criticism in these matters, after Lord Cochrane had made his escape and so called the whole system into question. Combe was writing on the Marshall's behalf. What more natural and sensible than to engage a debtor so experienced in presenting the troubles of others as if they were his own, to defend the prison system? Especially when his own privilege might be under fire. It was the strangest writing commission in Combe's long service life.

On the whole, having partly overcome or denied the humiliation, his prison years were the best he knew – having no taste for common dissipation (always a water-drinker) or for travelling in the places he fluently described; not needing family life because so thoroughly failing in that direction, but free to wander, visit, dine and receive. In one prison episode we see him most clearly, for Combe was driven mad by noisy children and nothing so defines the life of a man as its minor irritants. Rowlandson's aquatint of the prison in Ackermann's *Microcosm of London* shows where Combe's rooms were, in the State

House, overlooking the outside world; but below him younger prisoners played in the rackets court, and children then as now loved to shout their support or comment upon a game. Combe found this such a penetrating nuisance that 'racket' must have taken new meaning there.

His complaints to authority, pained and restrained, on this theme are nearer the true voice of feeling than most of what he wrote – and show him, struggling against adversity in his room, the elderly artist unable to defeat distraction.

I am not going to make a charge against the general conduct of the children within the walls – that is an evil which must in time cure itself – but against one particular Item of it, of which I feel the hourly annoyance. – On the racket Grounds beneath my window, Children are employed by the Racket Masters, as it is called, to cry the Game:– of which I can give you a very clear Idea by supposing, a Chimney Sweeper, a Sprat woman, or any person engaging in those vociferating occupations, were to be crying their respective trades under your window. – I say nothing upon the effect of bringing up children in this way, – that is not the worst way in which these unhappy Urchins are brought up in this place. My complaint is that such a noise is made by them, who have no right to be in the place, to the disturbance of those who are compelled to be there. – But it appears to me, that the Racket Masters, are the Masters of the Place, and the Protectors of the Children in all their noise, riotous behaviour & impudence, in defiance of any orders of Yours. – I have complained frequently to Mr. Morris, – and he has promised that I should hear no more of it:– but his remonstrance is treated with contempt, and I have been personally insulted in consequence of it, – and the other evening I was saluted with the title of the Bloody old Thief, who wanted to turn out the Boys. – At this very moment ½ past 8, – seven Boys are playing at Rackets with much hallooing &c – under my window & some of them have been so engaged since seven o Clock of which event the Watchman must know; who, if he did his Duty should inform You. But this by the way, – the subject of my complaint, is the crying the Game by these unhappy Boys, Mr. Morris if you think proper, will explain it; as I have pointed it out to him while he has been in my room. – It strikes every visitor of mine, as an intolerable evil, – it has always been bad, but it is now become worse than ever; and as the days are getting long, & I shall probably continue here, if I live through the Summer, I trouble you with the hope, that your offices will receive such directions, as you may think proper to relieve me from the useless and idle Interruptions of which I have been compelled to complain; and which will, in fact be beneficial to the Children whose injurious Occupation I wish to interrupt.

It is one of several similar preparations; laced with a little special-pleading, when he suggests the boys will themselves be better off if rescued from their 'injurious' but obviously happy 'crying of the game'. This was his way, as when he pleaded for Ackermann against a tax on lithographic stones, that their present return was not yet ripe for swingeing revenue if such were imposed. Yet he provides a living self-portrait from that evening of early summer in King's Bench prison; the Bloody old Thief writing in his three-quarters filled-up pages, terribly distracted but making prose which is forever Combe, not playing arpeggios for the solo artist.

8

A Victorian Dining Club:
Ye Sette of Odd Volumes

Years ago in Frank Kermode's room at University College, London, when he was Professor of English there, I remember seeing an oak Victorian Gothic bookcase, with the legend carved rounds its doors, YE SETTE OF ODD VOLUMES; and inside, tempting rows of little books. 'What an enviable thing to have in one's room' I said. 'Oh do you think so?' Frank answered, 'why don't you take it away then? I can't stand it'. I wish I had removed then and there those archives of the Sette, left by his predecessor in the chair of English, Hugh Smith who had lately died. The seed was sown, and by one of those bookish chances which are not accidents at all I would one day have at home a comparable collection.

I felt the attraction of this Victorian peccadillo and the congenial nature of its members; of about three hundred and fifty little publications and bits and pieces, including the eloquent menus of digested dinners, relating to that society which called itself and goes by the archaic phrase, 'Ye Sette of Odd Volumes'. Here are the first hundred of its Opuscula, 1880 to 1939, starting with a little book of which at first only twenty-five copies were printed about their founding president Bernard Quaritch. A similar number of their Booklets fills one box, their thirty-five substantial Year Books a couple more; the Miscellanies run in sequence from one to twenty; the box of Occasional Publications should be explored, and a considerable assembly of evocative Menus. Now I have no more thought towards reading and noting the lot, than of experimentally eating even a sample of those colossal dinners; but what distraction could be more peaceful than to stay and look a little at that small company of

75

diners and talkers, taking themselves so seriously as to invent protective ceremony, united by books and friendship, the Sette of Odd Volumes?

They exist and continue, thrive probably; I have courteously been invited and look forward to going as a guest to join them, but for this essay the experience would not be necessary; I should like to recall that Victorian and Edwardian earnestness which had changed course already towards wit and ingenuity by the time Vyvyan Holland became President in the nineteen-twenties. I wish to get at old Bernard Quaritch in these little books, without overtone of whatever happened later; to know what it was like to join his circle, and share the microcosm they invented. Yet we should go first to a more recent occasion, November the 26th, 1935, when Bro. Ralph Straus, Scribbler & Keeper of Ye Archives to Ye Sette, delivered his address which the Chiswick Press printed, 'to be had of No Boke-Sellers' the title page tells us, 'An Odd Note on Ye Founding and Early History of Ye Sette of Odd Volumes'.

From the start it is clear that they differed in many ways from their future cousin, the Club of Odd Volumes in Boston; forever printing their papers, Year Books, Opuscula, Inaugural Addresses, providing their expansive and expensive but negligible footnote to learning. This is not value judgement, but mere distinction; the Club in Boston has also its record of publication. In London they nursed their creation, made strict rules, watched its development as if it all greatly mattered. Bro. Straus's record of how they began exposes their roots in that bachelor borderland from which club life was conceived, the convivial chop-house. About the year 1870 he tells us,

> three London tradesmen, all of them bookish men, were in the habit of taking their midday meal in a now defunct house of call known as Bertolini's Restaurant. They did not know one another, and they might never have known one another had not one of them, some time in 1872, announced in a burst of understandable enthusiasm, that he had become a proud father. Mutual introductions followed, and in this way Bernard Quaritch, the celebrated bookseller, William Mort Thompson, who could write a neat set of verses when he liked, and Edward Renton, an expert in intaglio-engraving, became friends and took to lunching together. In course of time they were joined by two brothers, Charles and Edward Wyman, who were in partnership as printers. Then in 1874 these five friends moved to Stone's chop-house, which you will still find in Panton Street, and there they were joined by Henry Bickers, another bookseller, and by Edward Lang, about whom, I regret to say, I only know that he had something to do with armour. The seven of them met

almost daily, occupying the same 'compartment', and, according to one almost contemporary record, there was 'much fun and displays of wit'.

Then one day at the beginning of 1878, that ever-memorable O.V. year, Charles Wyman proposed the formation of a permanent Club. The suggestion was received with what we now call acclamation, and there and then a discussion took place about the name of the club, the necessary rules, and the titles to be borne by its members. It was left to Bernard Quaritch, after looking round his own book-shelves, to suggest the word 'ODD VOLUMES', and within a few days Charles Wyman had printed a first preliminary draft of the rules.

Quaritch from the start was the man who mattered, who nurtured this child of his later years and found peace in it. Not that his life lacked fun, or the kind of 'burden' responsible men complain about who love it and would deeply resent its surrender. 'This year', he tells the Sette in 1882 after election to a second term of office as President, 'will be a very trying one for me, as so many valuable libraries of rare books will be thrown upon the market; nevertheless I promise you my brethren I shall always have the welfare of the Sette in my mind; I shall do what I can to knit us more closely together, to keep up the high intellectual tone of our meetings, and to diversify the proceedings of each meeting'.

So there was the concept of burden in Victorian business London: welfare of the Sette which must be knit more closely together, and so many valuable libraries of rare books thrown upon the market. Quaritch loved his life with the Sette of course. His essay on Palaeography privately printed in 1894, illustrated with twenty-five facsimiles of illuminated manuscript leaves chromo-lithographed by Griggs, was 'dedicated to my excellent Friend Brother Alexander T. Hollingsworth, Artificer, and President of The Odd Volumes, 1893–4, and to The Brethren of the Sette, with which I have been united since 1878 in O. V. Bond'. This tall octavo, as we learn from the title page, was 'Extended from a Lecture, delivered at a Conversazione of the Sette of Odd Volumes, at the Galleries of the Royal Institute of Painters in Water Colours, 12th December, 1893.' He limited it to one hundred and ninety-nine copies, a number much in the Odd Volume tradition.

The Rules they devised in 1878 were printed in 1883, volume three of the Opuscula, page 9, and I take them from there though Ralph Straus says Wyman printed a preliminary draft upon their first devising. We shall return to this 1883 Opusculum, 'Imprynted by Bro. C. W. H. Wyman, Typographer to ye Sette', edition limited to one hundred and fifty copies. It is our first report of the Club. The rules from 1878, apart from practicalities of meeting and subscription, were directed very clearly against bores. 'No Odd Volume to talk unasked', we read, 'on any subject he understands, – i.e., to leave *shop* at home'. 'Any Odd Volume losing his temper at one of the meetings', rule nine says, 'to be fined by the President the sum of 5s.' Two more from those first twelve should be quoted: 'Discussions about Religion and Politics to be put down by the President', and 'One Odd Volume giving to another Odd Volume unasked advice to be fined 5s.'

All quite unexceptionable and appealing rules, a touch under-graduate, surprising perhaps from these middle-aged men of business in late Victorian London. Those first founding five, one feels, had the right ideas, along with the mild whimsy of rule six: 'All *Odd* numbers to count as *even*'; which confounded Ralph Straus, but I take to mean eccentricity would be tolerated as a norm.

These we may compare with a later printing of the rules in the first of their Booklet series, 1890. Their number has grown from twelve to twenty-one – deliberately, we guess: 'The Sette of Odd Volumes' is itself now 'to consist of twenty-one, this being the number of volumes of the Variorum Shakespeare of 1821; but Supplemental O. V.s to the number of Twenty-one are to be elected, and to be incorporated in the Sette as vacancies arise'. Rather more formality enters as to election and subscription; as 'the first toast at every Meeting', is 'to be the National expression of loyalty, "Her Majesty the Queen"', we sense a departure from frivolity. One agreeable addition in the old spirit reads: 'No O. V.s speech to last longer than three minutes, if, however, the inspired O. V. has any more to say, he may proceed until his voice is drowned in the general applause'.

This must have referred to discussion following a paper; for the great development in those dozen years since the first five started had been this habit whose results proliferated in the little printed books. Indeed, Rule Seven from 1890 reads: 'Every new Odd Volume shall be expected, within a reasonable period of the date of his admission, to make a literary, scientific, or artistic contribution to the Sette'.

It is time to choose a few and examine them, and so come slap against the first brick barrier of books. These charming little fellows with strange names are reminiscent of the Daniel Press with printed covers of paper or vellum, boards occasionally, their endearing themes from those far-off evenings: Blue China, Sweating Sickness, Chiromancy, Queen Ann's Musick, Frost Fairs on the Thames, Neglected Frescoes in Northern Italy, An Old Stuart Genealogy; I cannot leave them, and am not tempted carefully to read them. All could be called moderately rare, generally limited to fewer than two hundred; they tended to be careful productions from Brother

Wyman, or the Chiswick Press, or there was that famous example from Brother Hornby of Ashendene. They have some age now, more than a century has passed since the five first resolved to form a Club. The truth is, each keeps its sense of occasion and has stood unopened from then to now. Often the friends receiving them ventured no further than to admire and preserve. I share their mentality, it was their approach and is mine.

Let us look at one of their evenings in middle distance, which must in most ways have been typical but in one unusual. They met at Limmer's Hotel on Friday, 5th July, 1895, to hear Brother Ignoramus upon the subject of Allegory: *Some Words on Allegory in England*. They always took odd names; Brother Ignoramus was Frederick York Powell, newly elected Regius Professor of Modern History at Oxford in succession to Froude. Max Beerbohm's pleasant design upon the front of the menu shows Powell with his notes at a table which has been cleared except for glasses and a champagne bottle, facing three books of unequal size which sit with spindle legs on the bench opposite. They did quite well for themselves with ten courses in excellent typography including soup and turbot, Escaloppes de Filet de Boeuf, Selle de Mouton Rôti, Poulardes Rôtis, with sources and salads and vegetable, before Pouding à la Sir Watkin. Vanilla cream with strawberry water-ice, a savoury and dessert followed.

That July evening his talk preceded a short discussion, no more illuminating than such ever are, which we find in the Year Book for 1895. Brother Le Gallienne (Brother Rhymer, strictly) 'said there were many points of appropriateness in the Paper. The O. V. were a sort of Allegory. They were an Allegory in flesh and blood, and champagne; and they might be termed a sort of reincarnation of the old humour, which was very much needed in these days of new-fangled humour'. Dreary comment one would say, from a fairly new-fangled writer. 'Brother Silvanus Thompson' (Magnetizer) with more enterprise 'thought it was true that, in general Allegories were long and tedious. When an Allegory was short, it was called a fable'. We get the taste of the evening. It had come some way from the conversation of those tradesmen in their chop-house eighteen years earlier: regius professor, author, scientist, the level had changed.

Brother Ignoramus was an unpredictable fellow, as Todhunter later wrote, and this time did an unexpected thing which disturbed the Odd Volumes and is my reason for choosing him. Common form among them suggested their small oligarchy would approve a gift of the printed paper after a successful evening, from which these many Opuscula drive. York Powell just arranged to get his printed, sending it out to his friends in the morning's mail – Odd Volumes and a few others, about sixty all told. This created at once some breach in decorum, and a bibliographic rarity. Quaritch accepted the shock with grace and called it Opusculum Thirty-Eight, providing a few Latin lines of welcome.

We hear repercussions in a Foreword by Ernest Clarke, Yeoman, to the 1910 reprint of Opusculum Thirty-Eight. None had before been reprinted, except perhaps whimsically the very rare first among them all. In his Foreword, Clarke says,

> As will be seen at once, this pamphlet offended against all the canons of the Sette of Odd Volumes with regard to the issue of its publications. Probably it never was intended as an *Opusculum* to take its place in the regular Series. There have been during the Sette's history numerous efflorescences of the same kind, which have been circulated privately, and have become sources of serious trouble to the conscientious bibliographer and collector.
>
> However this may be, our *Librarian*, Brother Quaritch, recognising the value of the paper but shocked at its unorthodox vesture, and unwilling to let it wander away without a label, promptly earmarked it as *Opusculum XXXVIII*. Brother Quaritch himself caused to be printed and issued a leaflet of 4 pages (not quite the same size as the Chiswick pamphlet and not on the same paper) with on page 1 the familiar words "Privately printed *Opuscula* issued to Members of the Sette of Odd Volumes. No. XXXVIII. Allegory in England"; and on page 3 some lines in Latin signed B. Q. ...
>
> Of this leaflet, Brother Quaritch sent round to each of the then brethren two copies: with the untoward result that after the effluxion of time a Brother, finding when he comes to examine his O. V. books, two copies of the B. Q. Title-page and only one copy of the brown pamphlet, may find himself consumed with remorse at having lost a copy of the latter, imagining that (following the customary practice), two copies of the *Opusculum* must have been originally received by him.
>
> A search in their ledgers, made at my request by the Chiswick firm who printed the book, revealed the fact that only 60 copies of it were ever struck off, and that these were duly delivered to Brother York Powell on the day when, in the characteristically Odd way above described, he issued them to the Members of the Sette (with one copy for the Archives).

So they resolved upon a reprint 'in the orthodox O. V. format, it being ingeniously suggested that the original pamphlet was not an O. V. publication at all' – or only, one would add, in the Pickwickian sense.

Clubs creating an apparatus of semi-nonsense must tread delicately upon the borders of seriousness. They were a bookish lot, inventing their small and ingrown theme, hence so many attractive but trivial little books and the need for complete sets. Completeness was ever at the heart of it, or they would not have felt 'consumed with remorse' in missing York Powell on Allegory, 1895, or its Quaritch title page. The concept had roots in that phrase of the Club's name, *Sette* of Odd Volumes. *Ye Second Boke of Ye Odd Volumes* appeared in 1888, one hundred and fifteen copies, printed by Wyman; 'Carefully Writ, Compiled, and painfully Edited by ye unworthy Historiographer to ye Sette, Brother and Whilom President, William Mort Thompson', who pleasantly explores its meaning. 'Does the title require a word of explanation,' he asks:

at least to some lady readers? Any single volume of a work, which, having lost its fellows, turns up in the sale-room, or in stock, in comparatively useless isolation, is known by booksellers and bookbuyers alike as an 'odd volume'; and it is a branch of the old book business to collect such almost valueless books, so that by the gradual discovery of the corresponding missing volumes, the set, or sette, may again be perfected. The members of this little Society, therefore, are not 'odd' in the sense of eccentricity or quaintness, but each is an Odd Volume only as apart from the rest, and the whole twenty-one meeting at a monthly dinner, thus united, form a Perfect Sette.

From almost their earliest days, Odd Volumes showed signs of growth towards something beyond mere feasts and papers and talk. They loved issuing bits and pieces, in which rarity could substitute very well for quality. Mort Thompson, printing his 'Straight Tips for the Current Year – 1881', added a few Supplementary Verses for the Sette:

Odd Volumes, of all sorts and ages,
I read in my prophetic pages,
Will all be perfect saints and sages –
  In Eighteen-hundred and Eighty-one.

The united Sette, on fit occasion,
Will convive, until articulation
Is lost in mutual admiration –
  In Eighteen-hundred and eighty-one.

And so on, never likely to have passed the mesh of literary editing but in context quite acceptable.

June 1885 saw the great innovation under his Oddship James Roberts Brown, of a Soirée or Conversazione. Brother Historiographer records it, in *Ye Seconde Boke of ye Odd Volumes*:

Our gallant *Librarian* took in the situation at a glance, and rose *con amore* to his full height. Such Mss. and such Books as he then showed not one of us is likely ever to see collected together again. The five thousand guinea Psalterium of Fust and Schoefer, recently bought by Brother Quaritch, lay there, surrounded by many not quite so costly, but even more beautiful works. The *Historiographer* hardly likes to expose his deservedly high reputation for veracity and accuracy to suspicion by stating the actual money value of this gorgeous display of rare books and lovely illuminated manuscripts, but the pressure of duty is irresistible, and he feels bound, therefore, to record the fact that the catalogued prices of the works exhibited amounted to £25,000; while there were many unpriced – perhaps as being priceless.

Now that might strike us as a curious footnote to history, for one rule of club life observed strictly then, a little lamely now, is that business and trade and shop get left outside; yet here was old Quaritch, taking in the situation at a glance as Mort Thompson charmingly says, turning out the contents of his safe with an eye to the main chance. In my box called Occasional Publications are three small catalogues, on pinkish or greenish paper designed with some care and gold-bordered, of exhibits of books upon just such occasions in after years. The first is called 'Exhibition of Manuscripts at a Soirée of the "Odd Volumes", at Willis's Rooms, on Monday, June 17th, 1889'. In an introductory note we learn about this group of books from the Hamilton collection, sold to Prussia before the days of control and returned for public auction in England, bought by Quaritch who 'is induced by the celebrity of the collection to show on the present occasion all his purchases at that sale, although some are of slight merit and value as compared with others'. And a note opposite: 'The value of each Manuscript is indicated in brackets on the left side below the title'.

One would like to know whether by such elegant opportunism Quaritch succeeded in selling anything. For two thousand five hundred pounds ('In any case the book is one of priceless value' is the mystifying conclusion to his description) they might have bought the Golden Gospels of Henry VIII, folio, MS. on purple vellum, written in gold uncials, in double columns, bound in old English red morocco, seventh century; for forty – one hopes somebody had the sense – 'The Monte Cassino Petrarch', small folio, manuscript on vellum, two illuminated borders containing figures and fanciful designs, smooth old yellow morocco, fifteenth century.

Somebody didn't like it, or Quaritch was sensitive to irony; in these other two catalogues for soirées the books are not priced. On 2nd June, 1893 Quaritch showed 'An Olla Podrida of Typographical Curiosities', in December 'A Collection of Manuscripts and Graphic Curiosities of All Countries'. It was also his habit after the close of discussion to pass round a book or two at ordinary meetings, perhaps throwing out some hint of value by way of conversational curiosity.

These soirées might turn into more and less musical evenings. On 8th June, 1886 after a discourse from Brother Quaritch on the Learned Societies and Printing Clubs of Great Britain and Ireland (to be followed by his printed list of them, Miscellany Fourteen), members and their guests suffered quite an ordeal of song, piano, horn and an un-named solo from the violin. 'Rage thou Angry Storm', Mr. Frank Ireson rendered, followed more gently by a Bedouin Love Song and Miss Violet Wyman's interpretation of 'Dans les Bois', by Heller. 'Only Once More', Mr. Jordan's horn pleaded. Several times more they had it, and the Musical Programme emerges, fully fledged, charmingly designed, Brother Burnham Horner its guiding spirit. Horner had a hand in 'The Lay of the Odd Volumes', that mildly deplorable invention produced privately by Novello as sheet music, dedicated to the Sette, composed by Paul Bevan, Ready Reckoner, for words by W. Wilsey Martin, Laureate. Nothing they performed that June evening of 1887 would be familiar to us now. 'Sleep on, dear Love' Mrs. Biddle could sensibly sing, without fear of Mr. Frank Ireson who the year before had performed 'Awake! Awake!' by Piatti. The Misses Nannie and Gertie Quaritch played a duet, 'La Luna Immobile' by Arrigo Boito.

We must not waste time on these nostalgic programmes and invitations to soirées of the Sette. George Haité prepared several with great care in the nineties, emblems of soirée taste in that time. They were daunting occasions, starting at eight. Tuesday, 12th December, 1893, at Eight o'Clock: 'The Librarian to the Sette, Brother Bernard Quaritch, will exhibit a beautiful Collection of Ancient Illuminated Manuscripts, and will deliver a brief address thereon. After this, the guests will be invited to inspect the Collection at their leisure, and the evening will conclude with vocal and instrumental music'. None of the Cockerell fuss about handling and opening Quaritch's beautiful collection. With voice and instrument as background, no doubt he mused about possible sales from this leisured inspection.

Music played too much part; we should leave it, and they could well have done the same. I would take as nadir the Coronation Ode by Wilsey Martin and Charles Albert Lidgey, Gleeman. Here is the Laureate's opening stanza:

> Hark! the rolling thunder of the guns,
>   Britain's guns!
> The mighty roar, and cheering of her sons,
>   Gallant sons,

And fairest daughters.
In our realm of many waters
Rulers in the Earth's four quarters,
Under many sons.
The King! the King! the King! God keep the King!
Our King is crown'd today.

First time those lines have been quoted, I would guess, and the last. I prefer Mort Thompson's piece for Christmas 1894, about a boat jaunt by some Odd Volumes to Margate, a high success which inspired several forms of celebration in verse:

John Lane, the publisher of works
Quaint, piquant, and poetical,
Looked, like his own framed yellow-Books,
Weird, mystic and aesthetical.
Dear Brother Quaritch longed to buy
The log for a memento:
As though 'twere some rare catalogue,
Or Missal *cinqué cento*.
Although he was not there, this fact
Is just as I've presented it:
I vouch for it as genuine,
For I myself invented it.

As to the conduct of the Sette, they had and for all I know have a few sadly foolish forms of ceremony, recorded in their *Book of Observances*; of which the best one could say is that it was ably printed in 1898 at the Bedford Press, upon hand-made paper and limited to seventy-one copies. A later edition exists, almost the same but boringly printed in 1929 by Billing, one hundred and thirty-three copies, the paper machine-made.

In the Quaritch archives there survives a box of Odd Volume bits and pieces, from its early years. Several documents there, including a longish biblical parody in manuscript, show they did not lack those vital attributes of a lively society, passion and dissention. A couple recall the tendency of Bernard Quaritch to display his own wares, the first an innocent letter from Richard Garnett at the British Museum Library, anxious to make up their set of whatever had been issued and proposing that 'if you can undertake to complete the Museum set gradually at a price per number to be agreed upon, I shall be happy to give you an exclusive commission ...' adding hopefully, 'It would of course be very satisfactory if the "Sette" would present future numbers, but I must not ask them to do so'. He might have asked till he was blue in the face. Quaritch for his part seems to have laid in a stock of whatever appeared, by means which remain quite obscure since each carried traditionally the legend, 'for private circulation onelie, and to be had of no Bokesellers'. In any event they sold like distinctly stale cakes, for a shelf of them exists in the Quaritch basement.

Another document, openly caustic, relates to this same theme; signed 'An Appendix Volume', not now identifiable but probably a printer, for this is set in type and dated December 12th, 1889. 'The Sette has been in existence for many years', he begins rudely, 'as a trade advertising medium for some of our Brethren'. He wants a meeting to be called, rules changed. He is prodigal of insults, which at this distance of years deserve quotation. He first questions, with deceptive courtesy, 'whether it be undesirable to consolidate the Sette in the person of Brother Q., to be called the Governing Body, and to present him with our small change and the chest of archives'. He then asks, sting extended, 'whether, if necessary in the opinion of myself and my old friends, somebody should not be elected as often as we can catch him, with the understanding that he shall do all the work, while the Governing Body get all the advertisement'. There can be no doubt as to intention, for it goes on: 'Whether having regard to the open-handed liberality displayed by the President pro tem. (poor brute), he be or be not requested to invest the sum of £10 (or more) in such books or books as the Governing Body may think good for him.'

I fear it was the product of thoroughly bad temper, deserving a fine of five shillings as the Rules decreed. 'Whether or what', his ninth Proposal asks, 'Advertisements may be in future interleaved in all publications of the Sette'; and the last straw, against which Quaritch has properly pencilled his one comment, 'childish': 'Whether, as the presence of guests at our Meetings has hitherto contributed largely to our success and enjoyment, it be not advisable to discontinue the practice of having any guests at all.' I speculate whether this might have come from Edward Wyman, one of the original five and still present in 1889, a printer. His offices were in Great Queen Street, and this upsetting document is headed Little King Street. 'Advertising medium', Quaritch writes with heavy pencil at the top before filing it in the proper place.

'Much fun and displays of wit' Ralph Straus recorded from those luncheons at Stone's chop-house in the eighteen-seventies. More in that spirit are a few jottings in Quaritch's hand, on the back of a German broadside announcing Otto Janke's Deutscher Volks-Kalender for 1878. The year matters, for we seem to be back at one of those merry middays, napkins tucked in and invention flowing.

They think up 'The Extra Club of Odds and Ends; An Omnibus for Small Wits, Punsters, Jokers, and every Body'. Rules were the order of the day – perhaps they had discussed the Sette's rules, and were relaxing:

1.   the number not to exceed 1001.
2.   Entrance fee 1001 farthings with 1 per mille discount.
3.   Anybody is eligible.

With their well-printed small books on hand-made paper, the Sette represented a world of the dilettante, the amateur and connoisseur. These qualities so struck a guest from Plymouth in 1892, Mr. W. H. K. Wright, that he recorded his experience in an essay privately issued, mentioning there the 'small and beautifully printed volumes, many of which are exceedingly rare, and sought after by collectors of literary curiosities'. Wright was there when Bro. Cooke read a paper on *Automata, Old and New*, including among exhibits one oddity in doubtful taste, 'a curious figure of a negro whom it was impossible to decapitate'.

With slightly closer acquaintance one becomes much drawn to the Sette and their Opuscula, from Bro. Edward Renton on *Intaglio Engraving* (1885) by way of Bro. Todhunter's *Riverside Walk* (1898) or Sir Edward Sullivan's *Verulamania* (1903) to Vyvyan Holland in 1935 *On Bores*, excellent chiefly for his quotation from Aldous Huxley: 'A bore is a person who drills a hole in your spirit, who tunnels relentlessly through your patience, through all the crusts of voluntary deafness, inattention, rudeness, which you vainly interpose – through and through till he pierces to the very quick of your being.'

With all its quirks through those years, the Sette was not a bore. With piped entertainment and every chance at home to observe the embarrassment of public people, we have less time for such a diffuse and merely sociable device as they invented. Perhaps this rather than inflation would explain the almost total halt in its programme of publications since 1939.

Their early menus make agreeable reading. What last-minute crisis at Willis's Rooms brought a manuscript change on Dec. 3, 1886, Cod & Oyster Sauce substituted for Turbot, Sauce Genevoise? How inventive they were in 1891 when Bro. Artificer addressed the Sette on *Blue and White Nankin China*, to think up such pranks as Purée de Pois à Chinoise, Soles Pekin, Asperges à la Mandarin and Pouding Glacé Tonkin! For *Ye Magick Mirrour of Old Japan* they printed the menu on Japanese vellum but refrained from witty food. A pseudo-Kelmscott device for the Sette appears in June 1894, but I like the comment scribbled upon one menu during a May evening the following year, no doubt as it came from the speaker upon his theme, *On Some Ideal Aspects of the Collector*. 'Collector is one who pays more than anybody else would pay for what nobody else would buy'.

John Hassall, Limner to Ye Sette, poster artist, father of Joan and Christopher, designed a whole series of admirable menus in the early years of this century. Now as we wonder what they thought they were at, arranging such careful evenings, recording most of what they said, we discover it perfectly deep-frozen with their menus which perhaps were better printed than digested. What was an elaborate London evening, in the years of empire? Why should we, or they, have turned out to hear Brother Cornelius Walford on *The Rights, Duties, Obligations, and Advantages of Hospitality*; Conrad William Cooke, Mechanicke to the Sette of Odd Volumes, on *Automata, Old and New*; or J. W. Brodie-Innes, Master of the Rolles, on *Scottish Witchcraft Trials* – to take at random three among their first quarter-century? Yet we are pleased to finger them, printed discreetly by Wyman or at the Chiswick Press, limited to one hundred and thirty-three or two hundred and fifty-five; for the truth is they created, made something from nothing. Out of empty evenings they invented little books. These, their menus and rules and dissensions tell us something of what they were, and we are glad to learn how they thought they wanted to pass a part of their time.

9

D. G. Rossetti:
A Ghost Story

There is a small strange episode in the writing life of Dante Gabriel
Rossetti, which has not received the notice it deserves. The story
starts with William Bell Scott's very down-to-earth account of some
astonishing days at Penkill in the summer of 1869; but it does not
end there. Rossetti was in a depressed state at the time – sleeping
badly, drinking too much whisky and chloral, fearing he was going
blind. Scott and Miss Boyd had persuaded him to rest at Penkill in
1868, and he went up again the next year. One day it seems he nearly
jumped over the edge into 'a circular basin called, as many such have
been designated, The Devil's Punch-Bowl'. The expression of his
face 'said, as both Miss Boyd and I at the same moment interpreted
it, "One step forward and I am free!" '

He did not step forward, but next day, as Scott says soberly,
'occurred an adventure more extraordinary than any I have ever
heard of in connection with a man writing his best poetry, painting
his best pictures, and exercising a daily shrewdness of business
habits, the wonder and admiration of all who were in any way connected with him'. It is easiest to begin with Scott's account in his
own words:

> But the circumstance I am now to relate, indicating the subversion of
> reason itself, it appears to me highly desirable to place on record. It is a
> problem for doctors and psychologists alike. Mounting the ascending
> road towards Barr, we observed a small bird, a chaffinch, exactly in our
> path. We advanced: it did not fly but remained quite still, continuing so
> till he stooped down and lifted it. He held it in his hand: it manifested no
> alarm. 'What is the meaning of this?' I heard him say to himself, and I
> observed his hand was shaking with emotion. 'Oh', I said, 'put the pretty

creature down again. It is strange certainly: it must be very young, perhaps a tame one escaped from a cage'. 'Nonsense!' was his reply, still speaking *sotto voce*, 'you are always against me, Scott. I can tell you what it is, it is my wife, the spirit of my wife, the soul of her has taken this shape; something is going to happen to me'. To this I had nothing to reply, but when we reached home in silence, by a chance which often takes place in life, incidents of similar kinds falling together, Miss Boyd hailed us with the news that the household had had a surprise – the house bell, which takes a strong pull to ring it, had been rung, and rung by nobody! Rossetti inquired when this had taken place, and finding it must have been just about the time when we met the bird, he turned his curiously ferocious look upon me, asking what I thought now? – a question as perplexing as the conviction under which he laboured! But I observed he did not relate the story of the bird to Miss Boyd with the same confidence he had shown at first, and when he saw she was altogether averse to entertain it, he shut up at once. Nothing more was said at the time, but we have thought of it often since, trying in vain to understand him.

So much for Scott's account of that day. Turning from it for the moment without comment, we can look at Rossetti's poem 'The Blessed Damozel', in the version generally known, which was published at the start of his volume of poems in 1870 – the year after that strange day at Penkill. And there is this verse in brackets:

(Ah sweet! Even now, in that bird's song,
　　Strove not her accents there,
Fain to be hearkened? When those bells
　　Possessed the mid-day air,
Strove not her steps to reach my side
　　Down all the echoing stair?)

And there it could rest, an account of a strange day written by a disturbed poet – except for some extraordinary facts about the dates of the writing of that verse in the poem.

Still leaving comment to the end, here are the dates. The first version of 'The Blessed Damozel' was written when Rossetti was eighteen, about May 1847, when it appeared in a home-made family magazine; and it was first published in the second issue of the Pre-Raphaelite journal *The Germ*, in 1850. Not many people read it there, and the best-known version – several verses added since 1850 – was the one mentioned above, the volume of *Poems* published in 1870. The astonishing fact justifying all this fuss and detail is that the descriptive verse about the bird and the bells was added fifteen years earlier, for a version of 'The Blessed Damozel' in the *Oxford and Cambridge Magazine*, the journal of the later Pre-Raphaelite group which appeared in 1856 under the blessing and finance of William

Morris. It appeared there rather later in the poem, and in a slightly different form:

> (Ah, sweet! Just now, in that bird's song,
>   Strove not her accents there
> Fain to be hearken'd? When those bells
>   Possess'd the midday air,
> Was she not stepping to my side,
>   Down all the trembling stair?)

So Rossetti had described a ghostly event in his life at least thirteen years before it happened.

Reading about it in Scott, one feels that the episode is honestly described and remembered. Rossetti's angry look, and the comment 'You are always against me, Scott' come from accurate recollection. He was not over-credulous in describing this or another equally surprising matter from that same visit. It is not for quoting at length here but the fact seems to have been that Rossetti's voice continued to be clearly heard reading his poems in an upstairs room, for several evenings after he had gone south to London. There is no doubting Scott's account of it.

It is surprising that no link with the poem suggested itself to Scott – who certainly knew 'The Blessed Damozel' in its earlier, 1850 version because Rossetti had sent it to him for criticism; Scott was himself a poet. It is unthinkable that the link with that verse of 'The Blessed Damozel' should not have occurred to Rossetti; but then he must have kept his counsel, and said nothing about it to the others. There were other things he had to hide from time to time, and secrecy became important to him. His character and reputation were unusually complicated in these matters – the bold bohemian *and* the preserver of appearances. It is likely that his breakdown after Buchanan's article, *The Fleshly School of Poets*, was due to this hint of the discovery of immoral love behind what was passing for single-minded mourning; the suspicion that not all the *House of Life* poems related to Elizabeth Siddal. He laid the scheme of publication and arranged the reviewing with an excessive care to secure approval.

Rossetti's was certainly a temperament which could close itself up, and keep quiet about strong emotions. There is nothing strange in his silence about this episode with Scott; or that when Miss Boyd 'was altogether averse to entertain it, he shut up'. And as for Scott, a phrase he uses makes it doubly clear that the link never occurred to him. He says Miss Boyd's news of the bell-ringing came 'by a chance which often takes place in life'. It was no more remarkable than that. Bird and bell were not naturally part of the same story for him.

Oswald Doughty, whose large biography of Rossetti was reissued lately by the Oxford University Press, assumed that the 'Blessed Damozel' verse described the incident at Penkill; he quotes the first half of it in a footnote about the day. It should be easily accepted that one refers to the other. The chaffinch alone might pass for ordinary poetic fancy, which Rossetti magnified when a tame bird disturbed him; but birds and bells together are too much for this, and the identification ought to be accepted. So we arrive at the next problem: why has it not been adequately noticed before? For it does deserve to be noticed.

Poets ought to grant footnotes more often. Unless one had read Bell Scott, that verse in 'The Blessed Damozel' would not be completely sensible. And as Scott's book only appeared in 1892, nobody in 1870 *could* have properly understood it. It has a possible poetic meaning, but not more – not worth adding just for that. But a critic who knew about Penkill could accept it naturally as a description written two years after the event. William Michael Rossetti chose to make no comment, even in his introduction to a special edition of the poem published by Duckworth in 1898.

But the brief reference in Doughty is even more odd, because he alone noticed the peculiarity in dates. No doubt he could not manage to believe in ghosts or second sight; and yet, if the possibility of a dream about the future is accepted, such a dream written down as verse should also be allowed. After quoting the chaffinch half of Rossetti's verse he ignores the coincidence of the bells. This is what Doughty writes: 'These lines definitely existed three years [he means thirteen] before this incident, as they appear in the version of the poem published in the *Oxford and Cambridge Magazine* in 1856. Possibly the incident with the bird at Penkill revived the original poetic idea which Rossetti in his nervous state transferred to actuality'.

But that won't do. It carried on the Rossetti tradition of shutting up in the presence of this disturbing story. It must be one of the most deflating footnotes in literary criticism. Doughty also quotes a fragment of a bird poem and suggests it was written at this time – though again it tells only half the Penkill story:

> This little day, a bird that flew to me
> Has swiftly flown out of my hand again.
> Ah! have I listened to its fugitive strain,
> For what its tidings of the sky may be?

And that is as far as the evidence goes. Whatever one's view of 'The Blessed Damozel', or of ghosts, one can imagine the private horror of Rossetti at Penkill, as he returned from the walk which had shocked him, to be hailed by Miss Boyd 'with the news that the household had had a surprise – the house bell, which takes a strong pull to ring it, had been rung, and rung by nobody!'.

10

Elizabeth Browning at the Mercy of her Publishers: A Century of 'Sonnets from the Portuguese'

Alongside that selfless love which must strike us in reading *Sonnets from the Portuguese* is a precision in the statement of tragedy, one expressed through the language of the other, as in these last four lines of the thirteenth sonnet, where Elizabeth asks him to accept that her state of mind cannot be put into words

> And that I stand unwon, however wooed,
> Rending the garment of my life, in brief,
> In a most dauntless, voiceless fortitude,
> Lest one touch of this heart, convey its grief.

Dauntless fortitude, because she will not burden him with her hopeless condition of defeat in illness; forbidding one touch of the heart, lest it contaminate his active life.

Modern editors banish the received story of a bed-ridden hypochondriac kept in the prison of Wimpole Street at the mercy of her tyrannous father, rescued by her poet in their clandestine marriage to live in the bliss of Italian sun. It was not such a tyranny, they say; not much in that old widower to complain about really, affectionate, possessive with an odd quirk of will which refused his children their freedom to marry and leave him. Elizabeth, one among twelve, had a happy childhood; the death of her favourite brother, mixed with a sense of guilt because if she had not persuaded him to remain with her a while longer through convalescence in Devon his death by drowning would not have occurred, together with tuberculosis produced in her the feebleness of defeat for which, the editors point out, we should not accuse Edward Moulton Barrett. His own business failures, death of his wife, reduced circumstances were enough to account for some degree of eccentricity.

Daniel Karlin, in his introductory chapter to *The Courtship of Robert Browning and Elizabeth Barrett*[1], considers the notion of Elizabeth's father as expressed somewhat casually by way of gossip in a letter from Browning's friend Joseph Arnould, and concludes:

> He was bad enough, in all conscience, but not in the particular way which Arnould's account suggests: his identity as pantomime demon was imposed on him by the fiction in which he, along with the others, had got caught up.

As to Elizabeth, the fact of tuberculosis replaced many years ago the fiction of hypochondria. Karlin writes

> The suspicion arose in Elizabeth Barrett's own family that she was malingering, and Betty Miller ... unhesitatingly ascribes her illness to repressed jealousy of her eldest brother, Edward. He, as a male, was to be given the privilege of formal education denied to her; she, at puberty, faced the prospect of relegation to the indignities of marriage and domestic duty. She countered by becoming a *sufferer*, a position from which she could exert power through incapacity, and which enabled her to evade the 'normal' responsibilities of her sex and class. But, though there is no doubt that Elizabeth Barrett exploited her situation along the lines that Miller suggests,

Karlin continues,

> there is equally no doubt that she was really ill; that she contracted a form of tuberculosis at this period, from which she was never free, and that she died of it forty years later.

William Peterson's *Introduction* to his edition of the Sonnets[2] shows a similar intention to replace myth with some simpler predicament:

> The Mrs. Browning of popular imagination was a sweet, innocent young woman who suffered endless cruelties at the hands of a tyrannical papa but who nonetheless had the good fortune to fall in love with a dashing and handsome poet named Robert Browning. She finally escaped the dungeon of Wimpole Street, eloped to Italy, and lived happily ever after.

[1]   Oxford, Clarendon Press, 1985.
[2]   Barre Publishing, 1977.

We should not be surprised at the enduring popularity of this sentimentalized story: it has, after all, the elements of a classic fairy tale – of *Cinderella*, perhaps with the hapless Mr. Moulton-Barrett cast as the Wicked Stepmother.

Peterson views Elizabeth's father as a generous and affectionate man, though his

> opposition to marriage by any of his children was, needless to say, a symptom of irrationality and cannot be defended as normal behaviour; still, on the whole, he seems to have been a likeable person who clearly does not deserve his modern reputation as the most awful of all dreaded Victorian fathers.

In this triple explosion of a legend Robert Browning's part must change also. 'Though the mythos invariably portrays him as resolute and firm', Peterson writes,

> the figure that emerges from his correspondence is that of a young man so inexperienced in practical affairs that he could not even master the train and ferry schedules for their elopement.

Both editors use the imagery of pantomime. If we may first rescue Browning, least equivocal of the three, from this stricture of Peterson for whom he 'does not always meet our expectations in the role of Prince Charming', some of us might find in favour of the romantic hero who failed the test of timetables in his plans for elopement, as a Prince All-the-More-Charming for his incompetence.

Despite the cool temperature of such editing it may strike us as both difficult and needless to kill the soul of romance in that strangest story of heartbreak and elopement. Knowing Elizabeth was tubercular, accepting that somewhere behind the tyranny her father had an affectionate heart, their history remains essential fairy tale. There seems no point in calling it pantomime. Peterson's satirical phrase, 'the dungeon of Wimpole Street', bears no truth because everyone knows she lived in an upstairs room and viewed the world from its window.

That her prison was private made it no more escapable; facing death, incapable of inflicting (in poetic image) her dust upon his purple:

> I will not soil thy purple with my dust,
> Nor breathe my soul against thy Venice-glass,
> Nor give thee any love: ... which were unjust!
> Beloved, I only *love* thee! ... let it pass.

Her father's tyranny, adding to the romantic drama, did not cause it and finds no place in the sonnets.

★   ★   ★   ★   ★

From Warner Barnes, bibliographer of Elizabeth Barrett Browning[3], we learn that by 1962 there had been one hundred and seventy reprints of *Sonnets from the Portuguese*. Several private press and limited editions had caught my interest, but a month at the Armstrong Browning Library in Baylor University offered the opportunity to witness most of the separate appearances listed in Barnes's bibliography and some which have appeared since that work was published. Perhaps there was never more vivid, even lurid evidence of the medium as message. My desk was an island in this lake of late-Victorian and Edwardian fantasy, a profusion of versions and editions, of floral decoration and forgotten taste, such elaboration and semi-daring oddity as would have astonished the author had she lived to view them. If the first impulse was to reject most as undisciplined vulgarity a reaction soon set in, of absorption and fascination among so many. This was the history of how *Sonnets from the Portuguese* had been read and imagined through a century since Ticknor of Boston issued the first separate edition in 1886; and for an eye too well accustomed to certain patterns of taste in type, here was a chance to enter a sort of art and design long ago dismissed. In literature and decoration alike there is pleasure in returning to understand the out of taste.

For about the first four decades of their publication, and about the last five, anyone concerned with the matter would have known that this sonnet sequence first appeared in the second edition of Elizabeth Barrett's *Poems*, 1850. A fact better known since 1934 than the content or merit of the sonnets, is that after 1893 collectors began to learn the existence of a private edition above the imprint 'READING: (not for Publication)', dated 1847. This little book of forty-seven pages, called *Sonnets* by E. B. B. formed the chief evidence and exhibit by which Carter and Pollard, in their *Enquiry into the Nature of Certain Nineteenth Century Pamphlets*, proved Thomas J. Wise guilty of forgery. The *Reading Sonnets*, as they have always been known, desirable for differing reasons then as now, were a vital and successful move in the Wise game.

I think we should regard it partly as a game. Wise created a lot of fun with his inventions, teasing the bibliophiles and as a splendid

---

[3] *A Bibliography of Elizabeth Barrett Browning*, University of Texas and Baylor University, 1967.

collector himself knowing their habits by heart. Occasionally he merely protected – providing special covers for a few copies of some pamphlets, which the collectors would then need as a variant issue – but his *Reading Sonnets* was pure invention. He chose well, just at the moment of take-off for this flight of sentimental fantasy in so many illustrated and decorated editions. The sight of it, simple and fugitive, offers a witty comment.

Before viewing the ornament, plain and coloured, we may look at those few editions which provided prefaces; for they were reflections of the mood, clues to the edition. A preface could be wildly romantic as the illustration. A resilient survival of absurdity may be traced back to Charlotte Porter and Helen A. Clarke, whose edition of *The Complete Works of Mrs. E. B. Browning* appeared first in 1900. Their introduction to the sonnets began:

> Reality never before flung itself at once so throbbingly and so exaltingly into any love lyrics as in the *Sonnets*.

and mentioned quite fancifully before the end such qualities as

> the golden intimacy of companionship within the house, the flowers and fragrance, the pictures and imagery flexible to every throbbing of living personal impulse ...

This essay must have struck a popular note, for it was used several times. Crowell's edition of 1936, reprinted as late as 1950, chose it.

Common to many issues of the sonnets was the essay written by Edmund Gosse under Wise's tuition and the shadow of his legend, sounding every overtone of a piece played lightly without much effort. Praising their technical excellence he gives a romantic account of what the poems mean. 'The tide of her unworthiness flows up' he says, 'and floods all the creeks of her being'. It suggests rather a conventional unworthiness than the interpretation which would see Elizabeth as seriously ill, mentally withdrawn, more unable to face his vigour than undeserving his love. Gosse mentions 'fluttering of the captured heart' above which 'the captor hangs enamoured and persistent, smiling at the fiat which bids him begone'.

In her excellent and sympathetic biography of Gosse, Ann Thwaite proves him innocent of the Wise deceptions; Wise had captured a valuable critic to spread his myth. Appearing first in Dent's elaborate quarto of 1894, the Gosse essay was reprinted with or without permission in each of the Mosher editions and, for example, in 1900 by the Palmetto Press of Aiken, South Carolina.

Elbert Hubbard of The Roycrofters at East Aurora, New York, never one to linger at the chilly edge of sentiment, could have been expected to make a meal of this. With him not only the poet but her fairy-tale grows sick:

> Poor little pale-faced poet! earthly success has nothing left for thee! Thy thoughts, too great for speech, fall on dull ears. Even thy father for whom thou first took up pen, does not understand thee, and a mother's love thou hast never known. And fame without love – how barren all! Heaven is thy home. Let slip thy thin, white hands on the thread of life and glide gently out at ebb of tide – out into the unknown. It cannot but be better than this – God understands!

Anyone with an appetite for more may find it, in this which formed an introduction to *Sonnets from the Portuguese*, 1898, or in its first appearance as one of Hubbard's 'Little Journeys', true or false, to the homes of authors he admired.

Two or three other editors deserve brief mention. Frank W. Gunsaulus in 1899, writing for Ralph Fletcher Seymour's limited edition, has nothing to say about Elizabeth Barrett's illness. After a general sweep through Napoleon, Wellington, the Lake poets, Byron and Shelley in three short pages we arrive at the news that 'when the year 1820 came, Napoleonism in literature was not dead …', and with some degree of vagueness it seems various new intellectual movements 'had created a hearing in the soul of humanity for Love's message and Love's revelation'.

If the rest seems plain sailing, that metaphor should be avoided because it killed her brother and after the tragedy of his death, which of course affected her profoundly, Gunsaulus tells us:

> There seemed nothing for Elizabeth Barrett than that the next shape stealing close to her would be death. But Robert Browning had become personally known to her in 1846, & though they had been charmed into near friendship through mutual tasks and characteristic achievements, Love united them forever, – Love as sweet as spring, as deep as ocean.

The pseudo-sumptuous edition published by T. Fisher Unwin in 1909 has a preface by Alice Meynell, enshrining a style which surprises us now like spilt treacle. Of Browning:

> He laid his happiness at the feet of something even lowlier than her mere womanhood – her most Imperial grief.

But Mrs. Meynell, observing the feminine stance of these sonnets, makes this distinction:

> There is a masculine and feminine in literature, albeit all men are not distinctively masculine nor all women distinctively feminine; because there is a middle way where men and a few women meet – an equal way of genius and of intellect. But at the two extremities is the song that a

woman could not sing and the song that a man could not … If some women have done more generally human work than hers, no woman has done work more specially womanly than this sequence of sonnets.

William Peterson describes the fact that a woman wrote them as 'perhaps the most startling innovation of *Sonnets from the Portuguese*'. For a wittier note on the same point we return to Gosse:

> It is peculiarly true that women who are poets can or will but seldom take us truly into their confidence in this matter. A natural but unfortunate delicacy leads them to write of love so platonically or so obscurely that we cannot tell what it is they wish to communicate. Not to seem so unmaidenly as to address a man, they feign to be men themselves and languish at the ladies.

A sober and unremarkable essay used many times was signed by A. S. Mott, a partner of Basil Blackwell in the Shakespeare Head Press. It appeared in the several editions issued by that Press, but also in versions issued and re-issued with black-and-white silhouette illustrations by Fred A. Meyer.

Among purposefully private press editions of the sonnets was the large quarto of which two hundred and fifty copies were printed for William Andrews Clark by John Henry Nash in 1927. Clark's essay for the occasion called *Some Observations*, makes the mistake of quoting Goneril's reply to her father's question (beginning 'Sir I love you more than word can wield the matter') as a fine instance of Shakespeare in a mood comparable with Elizabeth's. No doubt he found the passage in a Concordance, and used it, remarking that Goneril 'thus sums up the intensity of her love'. Clark was also very proud of his *Reading Sonnets*, not then knowing it as a forgery, but he cannot be blamed for that; and now the Clark Library will again be delighted to own it. Indeed the satisfied comment of his *Bibliographical Note* is true now as then: 'It is one of the scarce books in English Literature and is much sought after by collectors'.

As footnote fuel to this history of changing attitudes and ornaments, we have Clark on the one hand quoting Hawthorne's recollection of a visit to the Brownings at Casa Guidi, in which Elizabeth appears as 'a pale, small person … It is wonderful to see how small she is, how pale her cheek …'; and on the other hand Dr. Joseph Mersand in a 1966 paperback reprint of *Sonnets from the Portuguese*[4] mentioning among possible explanations of the title 'that the warm Italian sun had given her a deep tan and that the phrase referred to her complexion'.

---

[4]   Published by Avon.

From quoted scraps there is no thought of offering a serious summary of Browning scholarship with reference to her sonnet sequence, rather of displaying examples which, like the illustrations and typography, show how variously this book was viewed across a century of its history. From seeing what the artists made of it, and in the light of modern frigidity towards fairy tale, we should perhaps avoid an easy temptation to mock the out of taste. The severity of taste, as we find it for instance in Mardersteig's bare-bones version of 1924, may even hold less appeal than a tall slim octavo with flowery illustrations of rural sunset, generously printed in green, red, blue, yellow and gold. Both, as extremes, equate and balance two sorts of criticism among the several quoted.

Though critics throw cold water, the elemental fairy tale remains. Nothing can reduce to commonplace this story of a brilliant woman who had given up hope and health, hi-jacked to joy and sunlight by the poet whose life she feared at first to wreck with her love. In these most private poems, shy and fastidious but breaking into the full flower of acceptance, nobody erred greatly to see the most romantic episode of English Literature. As another woman, Fannie Ratchford, wrote fancifully in the *Variorum Edition*[5], 'all lovers everywhere, actual or potential, identify Elizabeth's emotions and thoughts with their own, hug her sonnets to memory as the perfect expression of their own divine passion'. And the dark side remains. 'Sentimental jailers reach the height of their desires when those they love become ill' wrote André Maurois of Elizabeth's father, introducing a bilingual version published by Brentano's of New York in 1944.

Anyone may read a poem as privately as he chooses. I am most moved by the minor chord of withdrawal, sheer impossibility, and its change to affirmation in her wish

> to shout
> My Soul's full meaning into future years ...
> That *they* should lend it utterance, and salute
> Love that endures, with Life that disappears.

★   ★   ★   ★   ★

Fannie Ratchford considered the first separate editions of *Sonnets from the Portuguese* 'an uncommonly ugly volume'. Published by

---

[5]   Philip C. Duschnes, New York, 1950.

Ticknor of Boston, it is a large oblong book measuring thirteen inches by fifteen and a half. She added, writing in 1950, that 'it apparently lost whatever attraction it had for the original purchasers, for it has practically disappeared from existence'.

In 1950 that might have been called feminine logic: the rarity could suggest it is a treasured volume which seldom appears for sale or that it was badly made and fell apart. Either way, it seems best to suspend ordinary standards of criticism in looking at these books, accepting them as in the taste of their time. We may regard Wise's little forgery, about six and three quarter inches by four and a half, ingeniously simple, as inspired by this Ticknor publication which began a fashion. The illustrator, Ludvig Sandoe Ipsen, placed each sonnet within large decorative borders recalling sometimes the style of Walter Crane. As each has its half title in a roundel and every verso is blank, and the gilt-edged paper is thick in the way of its day, this becomes not only the first separate version but the stoutest. Printed sepia, all lettering is in drawn capitals. The artist signing within several borders, was probably responsible for every aspect of design. We see his work upon the cover too, title against the panel of gold which seems to disintegrate in a tangle of ribbons. Heavy to handle, much read in its day and printed on brittle paper, we cannot feel surprised if many copies disintegrated in the century which followed.

Also from Boston came in the same year a good-taste edition, as we might now view it, published by Lathrop and edited with notes by W. J. Rolfe. This rational quarto, seven inches by eight and a quarter, again uses only the recto of each leaf. Printed in sepia (characteristic of that moment, why not?) with sensible two-line initials in red, Lathrop produced their quiet reply to Ticknor. It was not a good period for paper; pages tend to break off as if cut at the inner margin. The helpful editorial notes are preceded by a short essay quoting at length from two other critics.

In their different ways these Boston editions of 1886 typify the two paths this poem would follow. It is tempting first to explore the wilder shores of love in a few editions with coloured illustration, among which I would choose the charming volume published by Putnam of New York in 1902, floriated in art nouveau style by Margaret Armstrong. Each sonnet takes a right-hand page, opposite alternating wreaths and panels which enclose more or less apt quotations from other poets all duly indexed for us at the end. A touch of additional propriety is given by lines from the Song of Solomon in Latin. Sepia for the poems, yellow and green and pink and blue decoration, with delicate drawings of lovers make this a happy book – as in sum total it should be. Flowers from opposite stray across sometimes as half borders to the poems, recalling many French books similarly produced in the late-nineteenth century. A little sentimental in effect but not in detail, one would like to come upon more of Margaret Armstrong's work.

A further flight of fancy is suggested by the tall slim octavo mentioned earlier issued by Hayes Lithographing Company of Buffalo, undated and not in the Barnes bibliography, probably from about 1910. Printed in a prevailing green, with liberal red and gold, each sonnet is headed and tailed by vignettes of ships at sea, launched by largish floral initials red against green and gold. Only sixteen sonnets are given (no note mentions or explains this truncation) but colour and ornament almost compensate. On five pages we enter the archetypal world of flower posy, cottage garden, thatch and sunset. I am not against this acceptable Christmas present from three quarters of a century ago. Illustration represents a response to the poem, not analytic comment.

In 1904 the Dodge Publishing Company of New York – interesting to note how popular this vein became in the United States – produced their flowery lithographic edition 'from Water Colour Sketches', they say, 'by W. H. Cuthbertson'. Again in a French way petals drop among the poems or brush strokes colour the background of printed lines. Dodge were less than generous to their artist in commissioning too few sketches, so several are repeated. Violets, poppies, roses, pansies, grapes make their random way through the book; a watery flowery scene twice crosses double openings. Not a distinguished example of its kind, the fruit and blossom doubtless helped readers through these deceptively cerebral sonnets to such triumph as

> I love thee with a love I seemed to lose
> With my lost saints – I love thee with the breath,
> Smiles, tears of all my life! – and, if God chooses,
> I shall but love thee better after death.

The green binding has a heavy bunch of purple grapes, hung below dark leaves.

For an early instance of coloured illustration, rather than decoration, we can look at a simple edition, small slim quarto, published by Jack in London and Dutton in New York, undated except by Herbert Cole the artist who signed and inscribed each picture 1907. In a latter-day Pre-Raphaelite way they offer, as an artist must, one man's interpretation of the poem; so upon four pages of art paper we find the healthiest of heroines in ballroom dresses, housebound or imagining herself in a meadow, surprised by the 'mystic Shape' at first (who turns out to be love not Death) and languidly swooning at last as a handsome young Robert kisses her hand poised above the flowers which might stain her silken lap.

With the Dodge edition of 1916 we are in an interesting phase of photography combined with real or artificial background. This quarto belongs really with the group I shall call neo-Kelmscott, but 'with photographic illustrations' as the title page tell us, 'by Adelaide Hanscom Leeson'. They come from their moment, giving a camera's realism to the earlier imaginings. It is mentioned thus out of turn because of the unfortunate decision taken seven years later by the publishers, to produce a luxurious version of the same book with its pictures 'reproduced in colour', as we now learn, 'by C. J. Smith'. As we see them by natural light or through waves of semi-transparent paper each seems more dreadful than the last. Patience ends, the appetite is ready for Mardersteig at Verona unadorned. It seems that in the history of this poem everything came at due season. The binding has a form of mottled leather with the viciousness of plastic before that substance was invented.

It has to be admitted that coloured illustration for *Sonnets from the Portuguese* grows worse and sloppier as the years pass. Two more examples will suffice. Crowell in 1936 issued a quarto edition, reprinted in the same years, illustrated in colour by Willy Pogány. This exercise in commonplace vulgarity achieved a good success, the lesson all publishers learn, reappearing in pseudo-luxurious dress as late as 1950. And in 1954 Doubleday's octavo edition offered art in colour by Adolf Hallman, of which it may simply be said that at such a date the poem was so safely established that no publisher or artist could damage it.

★　★　★　★　★

Though the habit of black-and-white photography from an artist's work would seldom now be used as book illustration, the Dodge edition of 1916 mentioned above explored it and two other examples are of interest. If Dent's version from 1894 is often remembered for Gosse's essay, as book production it still holds our attention. 'Printed in Phototype', we read at the end, 'by J. Löwy of Vienna'. As was common in publications of this sort the poems were written, not type-set, within the artist's illustrative panels and everything photographed together, printed as one process. The result may now strike us as less than stirring, but made with intellectual care.

Following Gosse we have an attractive essay by the illustrator, Frederick Colin Tilney, who viewed the problem which faced him. 'While poetry which is full of incident', he writes,

> and items of tangibility can take illustrative art with it step by step, the poetry that is not epic, but abstract and introspective, defies illustration in the most ordinary sense of the word: as when a poet speaks of the conditions or sensations of his mind, a subject which in its bare predication eludes the draughtsman's pencil, as much as does the scent of the honeysuckle. This being so, it is evident that where the poet goes the artist cannot always follow. When the one will spread wings and soar into the domain of spirit, the other must remain always in the world of matter.

Thus he expressed the dilemma of any artist illustrating any poem which is not a mere story of action, or epic. Recognising that in these sonnets the only action was Elizabeth's existence in Wimpole Street, and Robert's visits, quite superficial to the mind's action (impossible to illustrate) which they really tell, his own solution was to choose action or decoration removed from the immediate life of the poet, not necessarily from one place or time either – Greek perhaps or Moorish, whatever seemed fitting. With the same reasoning he almost abandons Elizabeth altogether:

> Indeed, so long as the poem is considered as a woman's hymn of thankfulness for a good man's love, with a recurring burden which tells of her own unworthiness, it is a distinct advantage to the artist to forget Mrs. Browning's own love-story.

In taking leave of Mrs. Browning poor Tilney also abandons most of the help an artist should provide – it could be said he hinders and misleads us. For instance in the thirtieth sonnet she compares her love, broken by emotion, with an acolyte who swoons on the altar step; so we see in this book a boy collapsed on the church floor, choirboys behind and the fussed old priest coming up to help; but none of this helps us respond as it should to the poem.

The dilemma cannot be avoided, here or elsewhere, of using direct image to illustrate an emotional poem. This artist knew it, and failed. Neither do we want to see Elizabeth attempting to view through tears the true Robert who had called on her that afternoon. Perhaps not one of her finest sonnets, it bore a weight of emotion no imagined scene could assume. Tilney's device provides, it may be granted, an *aide-mémoire* for what we have read.

The Fisher Unwin edition, 1909, following a method similar to Dent's in 1894, was reproduced photographically from a manuscript written and illuminated by Nestore Leoni. Both versions had notable introductions, Dent's by Gosse and Unwin's by Alice Meynell.

Nestore Leoni's original manuscript must exist somewhere, with its many rich borders in the manner of an opulent Italian humanist work, but reproduced in dark sepia the mood changes from Italian sunlight to London of the Edwardian era in winter. Each sonnet is beneath a small reproduction of some work of art, generally Italian and always scrupulously identified. Nestore Leoni was also responsible for illuminating a rich quarto printed on vellum in a small edition of thirty copies, published by George D. Sproul in 1902. Her Italian humanist initials to each sonnet are both scholarly and beautiful, but coarse typography almost defeats them.

★   ★   ★   ★   ★

With these out of the way we are free to look at the last, easiest group which I have called neo-Kelmscott. The Kelmscott Press, William Morris's powerful attempt to change prevailing standards in book production, thrived from 1891 when its first book appeared until the death of Morris in 1896. The press continued for two more years, completing work which was already sufficiently advanced. The idea was a return to earlier centuries, preferably the fifteenth when printing began, to use fine paper, adopting and adapting old type forms to achieve strong impressions again with the right ink. If the formula sounds simple it needed the knowledge and energy of genius, and over a long period of book production it made something like the effect intended. It also caused many an erratic exercise in strange taste, for Morris never meant his particular style of design to be imitated.

The functions of decoration and illustration in these books provide a perennially interesting theme. If it was impossible to illustrate *Sonnets from the Portuguese*, design could help as abstract art. The comparison should not be pressed too far, for a printer's equipment might serve many different texts, but design and type both contribute to the reader's response. A private press edition could create those overtones an artist's images might fail to achieve.

An early instance of the kind came from Copeland and Day of Boston in 1896. Notable for copying the Kelmscott designs, here we find one of Morris's large alphabets of initials and a vine border faithfully plagiarised. Whether Morris wanted that or not the effect, less admirable than in its model, appeals to us now. Seven hundred and fifty were printed, with 'ornamental designs', the colophon rather mendaciously tells us, by Bertram Grosvenor Goodhue. One year later came the Vale Press edition, faithful but original in the Morris tradition, a little book designed by Charles Ricketts, Oscar Wilde's friend who also designed *The Sphinx* and *House of Pomegranates* for Wilde. This is perhaps the best performance, in a turn-of-the-century style, of *Sonnets from the Portuguese.*

To go through them chronologically is easiest. Thomas Mosher of Portland, Maine, produced several editions of which the first, 1897, was best and with or without permission Gosse's preface was used. Mosher called the group in which this appeared his Old World Series. Elbert Hubbard also printed several, 'at the Roycroft Shop that is in E. Aurora, New York', the first a large quarto in 1898. When Hubbard sank with the *Lusitania* the world lost a curious mix of humbug and devotion to art. If Roycrofters represent a sick end of the arts-and-crafts spectrum, good paper and steadfast ideals went some way towards redeeming them. Blue and red initials copied from German incunabula bear no relation to Elizabeth Browning's poems – but, they had had nothing to do with St. Augustine or the Bible either. We have no proper cause for complaint.

It is interesting to find the Chiswick Press in 1898 copying Kelmscott as had Copeland and Day. The title opening at least is imitative. J. A. Duncan and Christopher Dean, according to the colophon, were responsible for decorated borders and initials. It was not in the best Chiswick Press tradition. Those who attempted fine editions soon turned from the immediate visual influence of Morris. Still in the nineteenth century we have a curious volume from Ralph Fletcher Seymour in Chicago. As the critical faculty grows lax after nearly a century it appeals now in a way, though it should not. Red, green and purple decorate the text which is printed from calligraphy. Seymour himself could manage a quieter book; yet one welcomes the moderately eccentric, upon good paper, and we cannot declare that it makes no impact.

In this high period for *Sonnets from the Portuguese*, two private press editions opened the new century. The Palmetto Press of Aiken, South Carolina, has already been mentioned as including Gosse's preface. With painted initials, on good hand-made paper as is the Armstrong Browning Library copy, though there were only ten thus, this was among the better editions. Its colophon uses phrases associated with phases of the private press movement:

So here endeth Sonnets from the Portuguese as written by Elizabeth Barrett Browning, the Preface by Edmund Gosse being a portion of an essay which was first printed as a preface to an English edition of the Sonnets in MDCCCXCIV: done into a book, after divers trials and tribulations and with much love of the work, by W. L. Washburn, at The Palmetto Press which is in Aiken, S.C., this month of November, in the year MDCCCC.

The Elston Press, starting on Eighty-eighth Street in New York, moving later to New Rochelle, printed in the early nineteen hundreds a group of simple and immaculate books on excellent paper. In very different style, within broad art nouveau borders of iris and water lily, *Sonnets from the Portuguese* in 1900 was their first. According to the prospectus, 'The type used has been re-cut from the "Chaucer" type designed by William Morris for the Kelmscott Press, and is direct from the foundry, this book being the first impression taken from it'. It may also have been the last, for the trustees of Morris's estate would not have approved at all and I do not recollect another Elston Press book in this type.

Studio designers, once they caught the drift of it, managed to copy or parody the Kelmscott look. For us it is difficult to discriminate admiring one or rejecting another, for Morris became the style of the moment. A graphic artist of that school was Adrian J. Orio, whose borders and initials decorated a turn-of-the-century edition of the sonnets, undated, published in London by Harrap but ascribed to The Colonial Press, Boston. He must have designed the blind-stamped binding too.

Though most of these examples come from America, Britain was equally held in the habit. A neo-Kelmscott edition of three hundred copies on Whatman paper, with dense title-opening and white-on-black initials eight lines high, was published by Otto Schulze of Edinburgh in 1901. Quite different from that quarto, John Lane issued a small tall volume the following year with green text and art nouveau ornament in mauve, one of a series Lane called the Lover's Library. These green and mauve lovers could there have found whatever from Elizabeth Browning could be brought into orbit, not only the forty-three sonnets.

The Caradoc Press has attracted me with its books, which were the work of H. G. Webb and his wife, its place, Bedford Park where Yeats lived for a while, and its name which recalls a steep hill in Shropshire. The Armstrong Browning Library owns one of several copies of their edition printed on vellum, 1906. Last of the pre-war decorated versions to be mentioned in this group was the Riccardi Press *Sonnets from the Portuguese*, 1914. This simple setting in Herbert Horne's type has a thick black title border but the Kelmscott memory was fading.

★   ★   ★   ★   ★

It is tempting now to break this narrative with a word about the origin and publishing of the sonnets. The Reading 1847 edition, exposed by Carter and Pollard as a forgery, set the Wise ball rolling as is well known. One new detail may be thrown into that puzzle, showing how hard it is so long after an event to interpret evidence. Without repeating each stage of the history now, their 1934 *Enquiry* based partly upon detective work with type and paper did not have access to a vital letter from Browning to Julia Wedgwood, unpublished while they investigated. Several different versions of Browning's first sight of the sonnets exist, three as told by the poet himself. For Julia Wedgwood he dated them clearly enough:

> Yes, that was a strange, heavy crown, that wreath of Sonnets, put on me one morning unawares, three years after it had been twined – all this delay, because I happened early to say something against putting one's love into verse: then again, I said something else on the other side, one evening at Lucca, – and the next morning she said hesitatingly 'Do you know I once wrote some poems about you?' – and then – 'There they are, if you care to see them' – and there was the little Book I have here – with the last Sonnet dated two days before our marriage. How I see the gesture, and hear the tones ...

The 'Little Book' was her manuscript, now in the British Library.

His date and place disprove the Reading Sonnets. Carter and Pollard had asked: 'Are there any references to, or bearing on, the book in Robert Browning's published correspondence?' and answered, 'We have succeeded in discovering only one such reference', in a letter to Leigh Hunt. Though they could not know the Julia Wedgwood letter they might have discovered another, quoted by Pen Browning in his prefatory Note to the miniature edition issued by S. Rosen in Venice, 1906. That letter is dated 1881; we are not told to whom it was written. The passage is worth quoting:

> The 'Sonnets' were only known to exist and seen for the first time by the person to whom they were addressed, two or three years after the writer's marriage. The reticency came of some misunderstood remark which seemed to doubt the depth and sincerity of such feelings so exhibited in verse. Fortunately some other long subsequent conversation did more justice to an exceptional case, and the next morning the writer said: 'Do you know I once wrote some verses to you?'
>
> This was at the Bagni di Lucca after the birth of her child a few months before. The poems were only printed at my urgent entreaty.
>
> I consider that the poor fancy that I might seem too anxious for my

own self-glorification, as people would perhaps suppose, ought not to prevail against all that power and beauty – however unworthy the subject they had been bestowed upon.

Had Carter and Pollard come upon this, it would have assisted their enquiry. The Brownings married in 1846: if the sonnets, so clearly remembered from Bagni di Lucca, were shown to him 'two or three years after the writer's marriage', they could not have been printed at Reading in 1847. This little Rosen edition earns its place in the story therefore, as providing the first true prelude to publication. Browning's recollections of her question to him, in the two letters, are verbally close: 'Do you know I once wrote some poems about *you*?', and 'Do you know I once wrote some verses to *you*?'.

⋆　⋆　⋆　⋆　⋆

The rest of the tale is quickly told. It comes as some surprise to find John Henry Nash, so early and in small square format, connected with a pleasantly decorative edition published by Paul Elder of San Francisco in 1910. Characteristic limited-edition language is used in the colophon:

> These, then, are the Sonnets from the Portuguese ... And the matter of this book was prepared by Arthur Guiterman; and the adornments thereof are the work of Harold Sichel; and it was put to press under the watchful eye of John Henry Nash, Typographer; and it was published to the world in the year of our Lord One-thousand-Nine-Hundred-and-Ten, by those earnest Craftsmen Paul Elder and Company, in the pleasant City of San Francisco which lieth by the Golden Gate.

In 1927, after the war and without those earnest Craftsmen, John Henry Nash did it again as has been mentioned; this time for William Andrews Clark and in fairly close imitation of Mardersteig's edition at the Officina Bodoni two years before. With Mardersteig one may as well close this account, though other editions continued to appear, soberly printed or in blue and pink; for that represented the bones of taste and any postscript to it seems trivial.

I have not attempted to show the whole history, but a fair sampling from collections at the Armstrong Browning Library. From it one sees what an amazing success was achieved by *Sonnets from the Portuguese*. If certain examples might have surprised Elizabeth Barrett Browning, at least she could never have described this assembly, in phrases from the opening line of Sonnet XXIX, as 'all dead paper, ... mute & white!'

11

The Pied Piper:
A Tale of Two Ditties

Perhaps the story begins, as is well known to those who know these things well, with Willy Macready aged ten in 1842, ill in bed with a cough. 'My dear Mr. Browning,' he wrote,

> I have finished the set of the illustration of the Pied Piper which I hope you will like as well as the others but I am sorry to say I do not think them so good as the Council Chamber, or the other one that I did. Hoping that they will be as great a success as the others. I remain your affect. friend William C. Macready Junr: May 18th 1842.

The four sketches he sent that day rest in a case at the Armstrong Browning Library, below the Pied Piper stained glass window; in my view a great success and among the best illustrations ever made for that poem, especially his drawing of the rats to the line he copied above, 'And step by step they followed dancing.' The piper, looking a little Scottish in his pied kilt, walks towards the river across a field which the multitude of rats seem to cover like mole-hills. It is a dancing poem, children have danced it across a hundred and fifty years since the date of that letter.

With it in the case is a note from Browning's sister Sarianna, explaining what had happened:

> In May 1842 Macready's eldest little boy was confined to the house by a cough. To amuse him, Robert wrote two poems which the child was to illustrate – 'Crescentius, the pope's Legate' and the 'Pied Piper'. At first, there was no thought of publishing them, but I copied the Pied Piper and showed it to Alfred Domett who was so much pleased with it that he persuaded Robert to include it in the forthcoming number of Bells and Pomegrantes. 'Crescentius', he did not publish till the last, in Asolando.

110

These are the boy's illustrations.

There we leave Willy Macready, son of the famous actor-manager who had produced Browning's play *Strafford*. He survived the cough but died in middle age, before Browning. His memorial at Baylor in the exhibition of these sketches is adequate, though it would be nice to see them in a printed edition of the poem, which ends cheerfully:

> So, Willy, let you and me be wipers
> Of scores out with all men – especially pipers:
> And, whether they rid us from rats or from mice,
> If we've promised them aught, let us keep our promise.

That is the moral of the poem, its message repeated below commemorative stained glass in that library.

Now it is a common-place of children's stories, that they digest comfortably elements of such horror as might disturb the censors of adult cinema. Another window existed in the sixteenth century in St Nicholas Church at Hamelin, as a monument to the same events, but it pointed a different moral lesson as a pastor called Litzner explained, writing in 1590:

> O you dear Christian parents, do not behold nor gaze upon this glorious painting merely as a cow or some other unreasoning beast gazes at an old door; but ponder it in your hearts in a truly Christian manner, and do not let your children run astray, so that the Devil may get power over them, as he so quickly and easily can do.

For there is such formidable repetition of the old story in one telling or another, as to leave a conviction that real tragedy struck that town in Hanover, seven or six centuries ago, possibly connected with plague, or battle, or recruitment for a crusade of children to Jerusalem. The number comes down to us with strange precision: one hundred and thirty children went out, and never returned. It is a tale of heart-break, turned to prettiness.

'Then,' asked a historian in 1904, 'why should not the historians and folklorists leave us our Piper, his pipe, his pied clothing and his rats, instead of trying to explain him away?' Pied piper and rats, but what of the children? Even rats, clever creatures, could become an endangered species and this legend turn to double tragedy. I seldom remember stories, but this one has no complexity: Hamelin is rid of its rats by the magic piper who struck a rational business bargain with the Mayor. Appearing from nowhere, he did it for money. Off went all the rats, following his music, and drowned themselves in the River Weser. And that was that, except that the Mayor, regretting his contract, refused to pay up. Exit piper, this time to a different tune which drew the children after, through a great opening in the mountain. It closed behind them. Legends and poems vary in detail, but that was the outline, here related with smaller art than ever before.

I do not know what the theorists and the Freudians say, to which pattern of tale it belongs, what need of the human spirit it may express – occasionally as a grandfather I may hope for someone to arrive from the blue and distract all children, but Departments of Folk Life Studies would make heavier weather than that. And the truth is, a more immediate mystery exists about this poem of the Pied Piper, almost under our noses, which nobody quite knows how to solve. I suggested that *perhaps* the story begins with Willy Macready, but perhaps it does not.

This poet was luckier than most, in having a sympathetic father. Robert Browning senior, working at the Bank of England, might have wished his only son to follow that example towards respectable commerce but he did not; defended him instead, after he was fourteen, from the trials of schools, supported him at home; and an aunt paid for the printing of his poems. Robert senior drew, wrote verses, was a scholar. Nineteenth-century England has many examples of literary public servants, politicians, tradesmen.

A touching treasure in the Armstrong Browning Library is the seventeenth-century folio given and inscribed by his father to the poet in 1825, when he was thirteen years old, a book called *Wonders of the Little World*, by Nathaniel Wanley. Printed in 1678, this collection of tales and legend has been described as 'a hodgepodge of historical anecdote and gossip, sometimes extraordinary, sometimes downright marvellous, now and then prurient or disgusting.' Much-used and lacking its title page, covers loose but about to be restored, on a blank flyleaf Browning scribbled pencil-references to passages which especially absorbed him. They are random and messy, not such treatment as librarians welcome now from readers, but precious because his – and among them, in brackets, '(Pied Piper 598).' The final paste-down has a similar set of notes, including 'Crescentius, 611.' In the margins of page 611, one reads Browning's manuscript draft of the short poem about the papal legate and his ghostly black dog, with substitutions and deletions, not published until 1889 but signed 'Done into Dog-rel, Feby 27. 1841. R. B.' After the fun of making drawings for that (safely housed at Baylor of course) Willy Macready had asked for another poem and received the Pied Piper.

As nobody doubts that Wanley's old book inspired this poem, his short telling of that strange story should be given here:

At Hammel, a Town in the Dutchy of Brunswick, in the year of Christ 1284, upon the 26 day of June, the Town being grievously troubled with Rats and Mice, there came to them a Piper, who promised upon a certain rate to free them from them all; it was agreed, he went from street to street, and playing upon his Pipe, drew after him out of the Town all that kind of Vermine, and then demanding his wages was denied it. Whereupon he began another tune, and there followed him one hundred and thirty Boys to a Hill called Koppen, situate on the North by the Road, where they perished, and were never seen after. This Piper was called the Pyd Piper, because his cloathes were of several colours.

And that is that, except for a couple of features which will be mentioned later because they find their way into the poem. Three more sources are printed in the small italics of a side note: Browning could recall using no other account but Wanley's and those three in the note – which already involved an exploration through Latin and German – but one appealing episode of the poem clearly comes from a fourth source not in Wanley, so it is assumed he knew that also.

Well, Wanley's report though more skilfully concise is almost as flat emotionally as my own. According to the author of paragraphs about him in the *Dictionary of National Biography*, this large book *Wonders of the Little World* 'shows omnivorous reading and indiscriminate credence.' It was a judicious phrase to use, 'indiscriminate credence' – belief in whatever he related, without scepticism or grade or level. That seems to define what a child takes from stories, acceptance and response within a narrow spectrum of emotions. These children at Hammel perished in the hill called Koppen, 'and were never seen after.' No nonsense about laughter and endless play, the magic of Kate Greenaway paradise; they perished.

But you can say, Browning adapted Wanley, did something better than merely versify the source. Before looking at his poem again, this may be a moment for exploring the mystery. In January 1890 a New York literary journal *The Critic* printed various recollections and anecdotes about Robert Browning, who had died the month before. Among them was this, taken from a London paper:

The father of Robert Browning was for many years – forty odd years I believe – a clerk in the Bank of England, where he wrote shoulder to shoulder with a man one of whose daughters married a brother of mine. To this fellow-clerk the elder Browning not only lent all his young son's early poems, but he likewise lent him his own MS verses. In this way I got to know, when a small boy, that Robert Browning, if he did not inherit poetic genius, inherited his faculty of rhyming from his father. In particular, I recollect a version of *The Pied Piper* written by Browning *père*, as being a very lively rhymed version of his son's popular story; and

I fancy I heard that the two versions were written by father and son in a friendly competition.

This fellow-clerk was called Earles, he lived in Hackney; and yes, Browning's father wrote a pied-piper poem for Earles' two daughters. Two versions of it are known in transcript, plus one holograph fragment which ran to only sixty-six lines. One other manuscript in R. B. senior's hand exists also, but none of the editors has been granted access to it. Browning's biographer Griffin quoted the first twenty lines of the fragment, and they are almost identical with the opening of those two known versions he completed; but below the fragment Browning senior wrote a curious note:

> I began this not knowing that Robert had written on the subject; having heard him mention it, I stopped short. I never saw his manuscript till some weeks afterward. R. B. 2nd March 1843.

So there is the father – we can call it Exhibit A – recalling that by curious chance he and his son, without a word to each other, commenced light-hearted poems about the Pied Piper of Hamelin. This is not inexplicable, or hard to understand. Those two knew the story well from its sources; there is nothing unnatural in the notion that they had talked about putting it into verse. I see the emphasis of that note as a statement from R. B. Senior that he independently started writing – whether or not he came to it first; that his fragment was the start of original work. He 'began this not knowing that Robert had written on the subject,' it was his own without Robert's influence. 'I never saw his manuscript till some weeks afterward,' so far from deference or diffidence, also reads like a claim of originality. Nobody writes such a poem without first plotting and planning a rough scheme, mapping it out. It is likely that a more substantial draft was made, which possibly still exists. Such is the strength and ease of the poem he finished later, that I am satisfied the track was prepared before he 'stopped short'.

Exhibit B is a half-known curiosity, existing on the flyleaf of that R. B. senior manuscript which nobody is at present allowed to see. It reads:

> This poem ... was written by the father of Robert Browning ... Mr. Browning, some two years before his death, told Mr. T. J. Wise (who showed him this MS. on behalf of its then owner) that his father wrote the poem while he, R. B., was in Germany: That upon his (R. B.'s) return to England Mr. Browning Senr. showed this very MS. to his son – who afterwards composed his own work upon the same subject ...

Now that falls upon the ear with noisy overtones, bringing back to mind the famous forgery perpetrated by Wise upon Elizabeth

Browning's *Sonnets from the Portuguese*. Here he is at it again, transparently.

Exhibits A and B flatly contradict each other: one says R. B. senior stopped after a few lines, after learning his son had completed a Pied Piper poem; the other says Browning wrote his Pied Piper after reading his father's completed poem. Browning's Oxford editors properly declare, 'We prefer the account given by Browning's father.' Wicked old Thomas J. Wise, successful in imposing upon bibliophiles a fake edition of the *Sonnets*, is here floating a statement that the poet told him 'some two years before his death' about his father's earlier poem. As Browning had died, nobody could dispute it except perhaps Sarianna, who might be ignored. What a daring venture, delicious prospect! Some sort of manuscript by R. B. senior was there, and still is. Would not a printed edition of it, the earlier version of a poem just then finding its way – like the *Sonnets* – into independent popularity, make a tidy fortune? Transparent now, irresistible then – but it never happened. Wise throttled for take-off and the flight was aborted. It will not amaze me, when the mysterious manuscript is revealed, if it turns out to be R. B. senior's unpolished early draft.

Yet there is a vein and grain of truth, to tease us; for if R. B. senior had mapped out his poem, and later completed it in the two available versions, that was no sort of imitation but dates from the same moment or earlier. Philip Kelley has been so dissatisfied with received history as to suggest that all versions were in fact written by Browning the younger, those in the father's hand being copied from early drafts of his son's poem. The most recent editors, to whom this suggestion was made, do not accept it.

Both the transcript versions of R. B. senior's little-known poem have been printed in an Appendix to the Oxford edition. John Maynard's Harvard book dismisses it as 'closer to doggerel than R. B.'s and spiced with bankers' jokes.' Nothing wrong with bankers' jokes perhaps, if bankers read them, but they were limited to half a dozen lines which come in only one of the two versions, and there is another interesting difference: in the 'banker' version, this is how the children heard their tune:

> The loveliest children in the place,
> Laughing – smiling – full of play
> Dancing to the lively measure,
> Following the sound with pleasure
>   As the piper led the way ...

Here is that moment in his other version:

> The loveliest children in the place –
> Maries and Kates – Essies – Bessies!
>   Full of smiles and full of play
>   Dancing to the lively measure –
>   All these followed him with pleasure …

Then the mood changes. My guess is that Browning senior showed
one version to his colleague Earles, who enjoyed the poem and asked
to share it with his daughters, but as they would not have understood
city puns those were deleted, and for Earles' girls it was Maries and
Kates, Essie, Bessies, rather than Browning's mixed gang of children, who followed the piper to Coppelburg Hill. In Wanley, you
may remember (and also in Verstegen) it was boys only.

The father's poem has been neglected. His was a rougher interpretation, the piper unmistakably (as in the sources) devilish, but
much of it goes agreeably, like this:

> The Piper then played – toot-toot-toot!
> Upon his more than magic flute
> 'Yes – I'm in tune (he cried) and now',
>   Making the Citizens a bow
> 'Just for a moment follow me, –
> 'And you shall see – what you shall see!'
> Lur'd by the music and the song
> The rats came scampering along
> In companies some millions strong
>   And left the town –
>   All of one mind
>   The roads were lin'd –
> Nor was one straggler left behind –
> Till they came to the Weser's bank
>   Then with a scream
>   All plunged into the stream
>   And sank! –
> The business was completely done:
> The rats had vanish'd – every one!
> Yet there was not a townsman's face
>   About the place
> But what seem'd blank
> Now they had Lucifer to thank!

'… and do not let your children run astray', the old pastor had
warned in 1590, 'so that the Devil may get power over them, as he
so quickly and easily can do.'

R. B. senior's poem brought back Lucifer, as of old. There is a
change, as the children followed the piper towards his hill after the

passage quoted,

> All these follow'd him with pleasure –
>   But with a tinge of mirth –
> Different from what's seen on earth –
>   Smiling ghastly – staring wild –
>   Leaping madly – roaring loud –
>   Each a monster – not a child –
>   Such was that fantastic crowd –
> Tho' parents no complaints preferr'd –
> Not one of all breath'd out a word –
>   – They made essay –
> But power infernal stopt the way –
> The piper turned from time to time
> As if he gloried in the crime –

Crime, not the happy heaven of Kate Greenaway from which a poor lame boy was excluded. And in this poem the Mayor was afraid to receive or treat with the Piper, knowing him to be a Devil, until the people forced him; but after the rats were drowned those same people turned round on him, for dealing with the Devil. 'We're ruined if these rats remain,' they had cried at first,

> 'And where's the harm
>   'Of any charm
> 'Tho' Lucifer himself should come
> 'With Horns & Hoofs to carry home
>   'His rats again?'

But afterwards they changed their tune:

> Now they had Lucifer to thank!
>   And the same crowd
>   That roar'd aloud
> To have infernal means employ'd:–
>   Now ask the may'r
>   How he would dare
> Employ the devil in his affair –
> Why not have let the rats remain?
> Wish'd they could all come back again.

It is a witty narrative, the Bishop blamed for urging the Alderman to employ Lucifer:

> 'Didn't I warn you all?' – 'not you!' –
>   Exclaim'd the Alderman – ''tis true
> 'You said the end might justify
> 'The means, & gave us leave to try –
> 'And if successful, then defy

> 'His works & Him & his queer clothing –'
> Then said the Bishop – 'Pay him nothing!'

Some slight hint of life for R. B. senior at the Bank of England is detectable in lines which follow:

> All this while the Piper stood
> Quiet in a melancholy mood
>   Outside the door:–
> The scorn of all the neighbourhood
>   And hooted at by rich & poor –
> 'Twas then a beadle from the corporation
>   Gave him an intimation –
>   They thought it fit
>   That he should quit –
> Could he do better than submit? –
> 'No' – said the Piper – 'stop a bit –
> 'Go back & ask them if they dare
> 'Bilk me of my legal fare?
> 'Give me my wages; I depart –
> 'And leave the town with all my heart
>   'But till you pay
>   'Here shall I stay' –
> 'No' – cried the people – 'go away!
>   'And if you fail –
> 'Here are the stocks & there's the jail –
>   'And know that we're
>   'Extreme severe
> 'On every vagabond found here' –
> 'Well then, if it must be so' –
>   Said the piper – 'I must go –
>   'But, only let me play
> 'One little tune before I go away!'

I must stop quoting from R. B. senior, in the conviction that the two poems belong together, neither written in imitation of the other, with ample narrative differences and few verbal echoes. Yet they grew from one impulse, the same sources, mutual knowledge. A Pied Piper book with both poems could be a delightful event; illustrated with R. B. senior's few sketches, and those four drawings by Willy Macready which have never been used to illustrate a printed text.

★   ★   ★   ★   ★

From Wanley's old book Browning took also the detail of dating all events at Hammel, as it was called there, from 'such a year of Christ, and such a year of the Transmigration of the children.' It is assumed that Browning knew another, earlier book with the complex title *Restitution of Decayed Intelligence in Antiquities* by Richard Verstegen, published in 1605. The lame boy appeared in Verstegen. I find him of special interest, for all this story invites some compromise between horror and sentiment, fun and disaster. Browning's poem offers barely a hint of horror, disguising its touch with farcical rhyme as when the Pied Piper first enters:

> Quoth one: It's as my great-grandsire,
> Starting up at the Trump of Doom's tone,
> Had walked this way from his painted tomb-stone.

No Devil, or fear of devils; no tragedy suggested in the children's exit. All clear, one could say, for Kate Greenaway and many subsequent editions, with their cheerful illustrators who had probably not read Wanley, Verstegen, Howell and the rest.

All clear for the lame boy especially, who 'could not dance the whole of the way.' What a subject for the children of Victorian England! Solitary, sad, shut out from the earthly paradise; yet – what really happened to those children? They came out the other end of the mountains perhaps in Transylvania, Browning suggests, following Verstegen and a later source, Collier's *Great Historical, Geographical, Genealogical and Poetical Dictionary* – though Verstegen expressed the scepticism of all good historians on that point which 'carieth little appearance of truth; because,' he wrote

> it would have bin almost as great a wonder unto the Saxons of Transilvania to have had so many strange children brought among them, they knew not how, as it was to those of Hamel to lose them: & they could not but have kept memorie of so strange a thing, yf in deed any such thing had there hapnd.

But the lame boy suited them well, is a key to the poem. If he missed a paradise we weep for him; if he skipped a horror, that was his reward and a lesson of hope for all sufferers. You just could not go wrong with the lame boy, who

> can't forget that I'm bereft
> Of all the pleasant sights they see,
> Which the Piper also promised me;
> For he led us, he said, to a joyous land,
> Joining the town and just at hand,
> Where waters gushed and fruit-trees grew,

> And flowers put forth a fairer hue,
> And every thing was strange and new.

Browning purged the myth of all unhappiness, as he had a right to do; thus we have the laughing rattling poem which has cheered every nursery from that day to this. He did more than purge, by introducing two charming inventions: the rat who 'stout as Julius Caesar,' by swimming the Weser survived to report the piper's tune, a remarkable music critic, as it sounded to the rats; and the lame boy's parallel report of paradisal wonder which all children heard in the piper's notes. Browning has a lot of onomatopoeic fun with his justling, bustling, hustling, clattering, his 'sound of scraping tripe,' his muttering which grew to a grumbling, which grew to a mighty rumbling, of

> Great rats, small rats, lean rats, brawny rats,
> Brown rats, black rats, grey rats, tawny rats.

Perhaps his father gave a livelier account of the Mayor's dilemma, of panic fear, but Browning added the light imagination and ('It's dull in our town since my playmates left') a Dickensian sense of pity.

It would take a bold spirit to imagine that anything might be proposed or suggested, in the Armstrong Browning Library, about Browning's Pied Piper, which had not been thought of, sorted, sifted long ago. Almost three decades have passed since Dr. Herring gave one of his students, Sharon Holmes, the task of examining and comparing the many separate editions which the library owned. Though others have been added over the years, the analysis prepared by Sharon Holmes remains a very helpful one. There is neither point nor time to view the illustrations across these different publications, in the way which struck me as appropriate for *Sonnets from the Portuguese* on another occasion, because those who made them faced no comparable problem. Browning's narrative provided the street of a German town, children, rats, an inflated Mayor and Corporation, townspeople, the fields, river and a lame boy. These, given and unalterable, arrived as stock scenes, traditional figures. Only the Piper was a puzzle among them all.

If most of these volumes look neither better nor worse than the run of children's books in any shop most days, that is perhaps because they were produced in large numbers on poorish paper. As so often, it is simplest to blame the publishers. In Parker's Penny Classics, not illustrated at all, a series of pamphlet poems 'selected', says Sharon Holmes, 'because they were named for study by the Illinois State Course of Study in connection with language and grammar,' the Pied Piper was followed not only by rats and children but by no less than forty-four 'Suggestions for Study', enough to wreck for most readers such fun as the poem provided; among them a curious question, 'Why didn't the Corporation get the money when they saw their children being taken away?' But one clever suggestion, the eighteenth, strikes home to us: 'Study the entire poem to get all of the details, then draw a picture of the Piper.'

I suppose that is what every illustrator did, and faced a problem; for Browning left them free to invent, provided the piper came out pied, sharp-eyed, dark-skinned, beardless, having 'light loose hair,' with 'lips where smiles went out and in.' So the artists produced their pipers, wild as hippies or persuasive as salesmen, young or wizened, handsome, crazy. As Browning had deleted the Devil, a light heart prevailed.

Only the first printed illustrations, for an oblong book issued for private circulation by the Chiswick Press in 1880, first separate edition of the Pied Piper, show a faintly sinister fellow,

> as my great-grandsire,
> Starting up at the Trump of Doom's tone

There has been no more impressive series than this, by Mrs. Jane Cook, reproduced without colour from her original drawings. The *Daily Telegraph* made a strange comment when it appeared, appreciating them for 'what is rare in a lady artist's work, firm, strong character.' A reviewer in *The Architect* remarked: 'The grotesque figure is instinct with power and individuality.' *The Sunday Review* felt this artist had 'richly and fancifully illustrated Mr. Browning's charming poem, with drawings in the German style'; whatever that meant. The Armstrong Browning Library has now reprinted this edition.

I do not know why, but after leafing through many decorative versions I return with relief to the poem's earliest and plainest appearance in part III of Browning's volume which was published in parts between 1841 and 1846 under the general title *Bells and Pomegranates*. Moxon needed additional material for part III, *Dramatic Lyrics*, as Sarianna Browning mentioned in her letter quoted earlier, and Browning provided 'The Pied Piper'. What is there in the crowded page of a first edition which lifts it above any later interpretation?

At the other extreme of the scale, Whistler's enemy Harry Quilter 'set forth' (to use his own phrase) the Pied Piper upon a flamboyant quarto page 'in a Series of Designs and Decorative Borders.' His wife's black-letter calligraphy, amply sheltered within them, set forth the text. Date and taste were 1898; an example, whose elaboration one must admire, of pseudo-Morris and neo-Kelmscott. The more extravagant copies appeared in bindings of green leather or white parchment over heavy boards, with embossed silver plaques inset, and ample gold decoration; some included full-page pictures colour-printed by Lemercier in Paris, upon both silk and vellum. Browning would have been, as we are, amazed.

One more example can conclude this ramble among the byways. A dining club still exists in London, called the Sette of Odd Volumes; founded in the 1870s, printing across many decades little books from the lectures and papers they delighted to give and to hear. For more than half a century the flow was abundant, always in small editions limited to about a couple of hundred or less. I find them an endearing assembly. In similar spirit Boston followed suit with its Club of Odd Volumes which thrives there in a charming old house and dines with no shortage of decanters.

In 1904 Silvanus Thompson, professor of Electrical Engineering and of course an Odd Volume, delivered his paper after dinner in London on the Pied Piper of Hamelin. A long sub-title on the small title pages, in that style I can only call tea-shop English, often affected by the Sette of Odd Volumes in its books and menus and forms of address, runs thus:

> Being an excursus or painsfull dissertation upon the Outgoing of the Children, otherwise Exodus Hamelensis, drawn from the original accompts of the same, delivered at the two hundred and fiftieth meeting of the Sette of Odd Volumes, holden on the twenty-third day of February, in the year MDCCCCIV, by the unworthie Magnetizer, Silvanus P. Thompson, wherein it is manifest how, Anno Christi MCCLXXXIV on the day of S John the Baptist, in the Town of Hamelin in Allemania, on the Weser, an unknown Adventurer in strange gay clothes, without doubt an Evil Spirit, went up and down the streets, and with a pipe did allure to himself CXXX children, both boys and girls, and led them out of a city gate into a mountain, where he lost them with himself, which hath been a grievous sorrow to the Parents, and a frightful example of the evil of sin and the power of the Devil: all compared with the original documents and the testimonie of the witnesses thereof, which let him that doubteth be condemned.

It is a learned little book, or lecture, from the professor of Electrical Engineering, 'Brother Magnetizer' in the nomenclature of the Sette, as good an account as exists of comparative sources for the story. Learned names – Erich, Fincelius, Weier, Müller, Herr, Litzner, Verstegen, Kircher, Dr. Otto Meinardus, and Dr. Franz Jostes – are dropped till they thump lightly on the floor. We may be sure this bookish society deliberated before deciding with what theme to mark its two hundred and fiftieth meeting.

Neither Browning nor his poem received one single mention through the length of the lecture. This was praise, revealing his Pied

Piper at the turn of the century, after two decades in independent editions, as so deep a part of normal consciousness that there was no need even to name them. Nine more decades have passed since then; we may now celebrate his poem for Willy Macready, without fear of exposing ourselves as commonplace.

12

Hume, Sludge and I:
A Study in Techniques of
Dishonesty

The wonderfully romantic marriage of Robert Browning to Elizabeth Barrett lasted fourteen years until her death in midsummer 1861, with only two dark clouds in their blue Italian sky: a chronic worry, which of course he shared, about her health; and a passionate excitement, which he did not share, in spirit-manifestations which rapped the tables of Europe and raised the pitch of social evenings in the second half of the nineteenth century. This form of fever seems to have arrived from America, and in a moderately classless way possessed the drawing rooms of fashionable and suburban London, Paris, Florence – even Athens, according to one of Elizabeth's letters. A high tide was reached, as it concerned the Brownings, in the six or seven years after 1853 when it became prominent in newsletters to her friends.

As a storm-cloud in the marriage it produced high tension, expressed in Robert Browning's hostile, aggressive poem 'Mr. Sludge the Medium'.

> Please, sir! your thumbs are through my windpipe, sir!

That is where Robert would have liked to press them: upon the throat of a Scottish-American practitioner called Daniel Dunglas Hume, whose excursions in spiritualism caught the throat of London – or Ealing, or Wimpole street – in the summer of 1855. The tension in their marriage is an interesting one to observe, and difficult to interpret. Quotations which follow are from unpublished passages in

124

letters from Elizabeth to Robert's sister Sarianna – other letters would serve equally but it is convenient to use these which happen to be present where I write.

Their acquaintance Mrs. Carmichael Smyth had a friend, Mrs. Brotherton, who claimed the gift of automatic writing – and, more than that, 'writes Greek in this involuntary manner, she not knowing a letter of the language!.' Elizabeth's comment, writing to Sarianna, was:

> Now, either she swindles, copying words out of a lexicon (and Robert has the courage to say that she does) or there is an agency independent of her altogether. Nerves will account for nothing here. For my part I don't accuse people of swindling or murder willingly, or without some previous suspicion of their reputation.

In 1853, after reports of wild goings-on in Wimpole Street ('They have all been moving tables in Wimpole Street with great success. Alfred, Set, and Occy with a friend of theirs made a table turn so fast that they had to run to keep up with it') she could declare to Sarianna her complete faith in such events, but Robert was the outsider. Elizabeth wrote:

> Respecting the fact of spiritual manifestations good or bad (probably a mixture of good and bad) we are all agreed – Mr. Bowers, Mr. Tennyson, Mr. Lytton and I. Robert won't believe till he sees and hears, he stoutly maintains, which is the more heroic in him in that he stands in a desolate minority of one.

When Wilson her maid, who has become almost as famous as Flush her dog, showed such ability in automatic writing as deeply moved and convinced Elizabeth, Robert as a sceptic was forbidden all access:

> Robert has never seen Wilson write, and I won't let him till he has smoothed down some of his sceptical bristles.

It was serious to stand 'in a desolate minority of one', when the focus was of such emotional power for his wife. I quote from letters written in 1853. His particular difficulty in seeking the truth was that this fish proved difficult or impossible to catch; for fact and lies, by an odd twist, became equally acceptable. An analogy with religion is obvious enough: God cannot be proved, as everyone knows; religious imposture cannot banish belief; lies may identify a fool, and assist faith.

The point becomes important, when we look at Robert's poem. It turned upon a specious argument, which Elizabeth expressed repeatedly, by way of defence, when nonsensical spirit-messages accused her whole system of belief: 'The fact of lies being told however, does not diminish the wonder of the hand involuntarily writing those lies'. Other-world spirits, like this-world people, could deceive or enlighten, spread fact or nonsense. The medium, it might seem, has it all his own way. We are still in 1853, but two years later a notorious event took place at Ealing.

The period is sometimes described as hysterical, fevered, ready to welcome deception from anyone who claimed special powers as a spirit-medium. Among such people, none was more flamboyant – or successful – than Daniel Dunglas Hume, 'who came of a family supposed to be gifted with second sight' according to J. M. Rigg in the *Dictionary of National Biography*. Elizabeth placed him higher, 'a descendant of the Historian's family, and related to Lord Hume'. A recent writer[1] finds that Hume's grandfather was Alexander, tenth Earl of Home, who died in 1841; his father one William Home, illegitimate offspring of that nobleman.

Anyway Daniel Hume, born in 1833, brought up in America from the age of nine, made a great splash at Ealing in 1855. As a very young man, 'furniture began to glide about the rooms without any physical agency being observed'. Among the reputable and less reputable witnesses who found his performances convincing, when he came to Europe, were Lord Dunraven who had every chance of knowing and sharing Hume's methods, as it is said he also shared his bed; Napoleon III and the Empress Eugénie; and William Crookes, later Sir William and a distinguished Fellow of the Royal Society.

It is now fashionable to mock the claims of spiritualists, as it was then to accept or encourage them. Elizabeth realised the folly and deceit of many. I suppose that if only *one* levitation or spirit-voice, among the many thousand, were known to be true, our commonsense view of the world would slide and career about as the tables did. Hume graduated, it is important to recall, from the relatively uncomplicated to the highly peculiar – though the whole subject, if not simply rejected, is complex beyond imagining. By uncomplicated, I mean furniture moving and inexplicable noises, as if announcing at least the presence of spirits unseen. In 1852 a dozen witnesses declared: 'The table around which we were seated was moved by an invisible agency ... The manifestations occurred in a room thoroughly illuminated'.[2]

But people who became too well accustomed to table-moving expected larger forms of impossibility from the extra-successful

---

[1] Eric John Dingwall, *Some Human Oddities*, New York, 1962.
[2] Horace Wyndham, *Mr. Sludge the Medium*, 1937, p. 37.

medium, and it seems Hume obliged more thoroughly than most. There was, for instance, General Boldero in Edinburgh, who 'watched, and saw his whole body elongated as much as nine inches or a foot ... He took both my hands and placed them on each side of his waist, above the hips; there was a vacuum between his waistcoat and trousers'.[3]

I am not concerned to trace Hume's life from the first sensational appearances in London, through success and disgrace in France and Italy, romantic and lucrative Russian marriages, and the courts of law where he was found guilty of improperly extracting sixty thousand pounds from a seventy-five year old widow; merely to point the existence of this surprising character, whose performance as a medium the Brownings witnessed at a house in Ealing in 1855.

Their responses then, as has often been told, travelled in opposite directions. The séance, at the home of a family called Rymer, has been reported in a puzzling variety of ways, but they all mention three curious events: a wreath of clematis, gathered earlier from the garden, shifted from the table where it lay and arrived upon Elizabeth's head; the heavy table where they sat rose a foot from the ground, with no visible cause; and the front of Elizabeth's dress bulged out, for no apparent reason. A fourth phenomenon, common to many of Hume's appearances, the fluent playing of an accordion which he held with one hand, seems too probably deceptive to have been worth much attention.

Hume's own account, printed seventeen years later as an episode among *Incidents in my Life*[4], is not without interest, though one may dismiss the impression he says the Rymers had, 'that Mr. Browning seemed much disappointed that the wreath was not put upon his own head instead of his wife's'. Parts of Hume's story ring true. 'Mr. Browning was requested to investigate everything as it occurred, and he availed himself freely of the invitation. Several times during the evening he voluntarily and earnestly declared that anything like imposture was out of the question'. So far, perhaps, so good. After the affair of the wreath, spirits asked all except Hume and Rymer to leave the room. 'During Mr Browning's absence with the rest of the family', says Hume, 'I was afterwards told by them that he seemed quite hurt at being sent out of the room, and said he was not aware that spirits could have secrets!' Twice hurt, and for-ever shy. Robert seems to have been irritated by the contrivance of a

3   Horace Wyndham, *Mr. Sludge the Medium*, 1937, p. 222.
4   Second series, 1872, *Mr. Sludge the Medium*.

wreath for Elizabeth, after preliminary goodwill, and properly scep-
tical in being asked to leave the room.

Hume's report of a farewell visit to the Brownings made some
days later with Mrs. Rymer and her son reads more convincingly
than the wreath-laying, and deserves quotation:

> We were shown into the drawing-room, and he, advancing to meet us,
> shook hands with Mrs. Rymer; then, passing by me shook hands with her
> son. As he was repassing me I held out my hand, when, with a tragic air,
> he threw his hand on his left shoulder, and stalked away. My attention
> was now drawn to Mrs. Browning, who was standing nearly in the cen-
> tre of the room, and looked very pale and agitated. I approached and she
> placed both her hands in mine, and said, in a voice of emotion, 'Oh dear
> Mr. Home, do not, do not blame me. I am so sorry, but I am not to
> blame'. I was wonder-struck, not knowing in the least what the curious
> scene meant – indeed, it would have been comical, but for the deep emo-
> tion from which Mrs. Browning was suffering.
>
> For a moment all was confusion, but at last we were seated, I scarce
> know how, when Mr. Browning began in an excited manner, saying,
> 'Mrs. Rymer, I beg to inform you that I was exceedingly dissatisfied with
> everything I saw at your house the other night, and I should like to know
> why you refused to receive me again with my friend'. I replied to this,
> 'Mr. Browning, that was the time and place for you to have made objec-
> tions regarding the manifestations, and not now. I gave you every possi-
> ble opportunity, and you availed yourself of it, and expressed yourself
> satisfied'. He said, 'I am not addressing myself to you, sir'. I said, 'No;
> but it is of me you are speaking, and it would only be fair and gentleman-
> like to allow me to reply'. Mrs. Rymer said, 'Mr. Home is quite right,
> and as regards not being able to receive you and your friend, we could
> not do so on account of our engagements'.
>
> Mr. Browning's face was pallid with rage, and his movements, as he
> swayed backwards and forwards on his chair, were like those of a maniac.
> At this moment I rose to leave the room, and, passing him, shook hands
> with Mrs. Browning, who was nearly ready to faint. As she shook hands
> with me she said, 'Dear Mr. Home, I am not to blame. Oh, dear! oh,
> dear!'.

He quotes Mrs. Hawthorne's comment in *Notes on England and
Italy*: 'Mr. Browning introduced the subject of spiritism, and there
was an animated talk. Mr. Browning cannot believe, and Mrs.
Browning cannot help believing'. Robert had brought up the subject,
which one might have expected him to avoid as a chronic irritant; for
it seems that from the first, when they went to the Rymers, disbelief
was tempered by fascination in the dark side of a mystery. Some hint
of false religion, of a tenuous connection with what pious people
seek, brought argument and consideration into his discussions of the

subject. As has always been noticed, 'Mr. Sludge' is not merely an intemperate poem. Arguments exist, which he could not resist. The same was true in Shakespeare's perception of Shylock.

Conan Doyle wrote in 1921, introducing a new edition of Mrs. Hume's book on her husband:

> Home is a man to whom the human race, and especially the British public, owes a deep apology. He was most shamefully used by them. He came as one of the first and most powerful missionaries who have set forth upon the greatest of human tasks, to prove immortality, to do away with the awful mystery of death, to found religion upon positive knowledge.

Unlike Hume, Robert Browning wrote his account of that Ealing evening within a month of the event, in a long letter to Mrs. Kinney of Newark, New Jersey. After 'some noises, a vibration of the table, then an up-tilting of it in various ways, and then more noises, or raps', they reduced their numbers and in this very just report he wrote:

> We had the same vibration, & upraising the table – a table-cloth, a few ornaments, and a large lamp were on it – all hands were visible. I don't know at all how the thing was done.

After the interval mentioned in Hume's account the heavy table was raised again: 'light was in the room – I looked under the table and can aver that it was lifted from the ground, say a foot high, more than once – Mr. Home's hands being plainly above it'. Robert confessed later in the same long letter:

> I don't in the least pretend to explain how the table was uplifted altogether ... and how my wife's gown was agitated ...

Browning went on to add however that

> light in some – & leave to investigate in others – of these cases – were necessary to show whether they might not have been explained & easily.

So it would be wrong to represent him as in any way credulous, even at the beginning when some sensitivity towards his hosts the Rymers, whose small son Wat had died and inspired them to hear Hume, prevented him from pursuing exposure and the truth that evening. Elizabeth found no difficulty in digesting all those events into her system; the graph of Robert's irritation rose steadily. She kept the dead wreath of clematis on her dressing table, he threw it out of Casa Guidi windows. Writing a note in the third person, he concludes

> no trick is too gross. Mr. Browning recommends leaving this business to its natural termination, and will console himself for any pain to the dupes

by supposing that their eventual profit in improved intelligence would be no otherwise procurable.

This is quoted from an article in the *Cornhill*[5] by Betty Miller, who added confidently, of 'Mr. Sludge the Medium': 'This long and acrid poem was composed during the last years of Elizabeth's life and never shown to her'. The point is of some interest, and much uncertainty. In *A Browning Handbook*[6] William Clyde De Vane expressed the same conviction, but without real evidence: 'the probability is that Browning would not have written this poem soon after his wife's death in 1861, so that presumably it was done before'. That gets us nowhere. Two references are cited from the poem, to minor occurrences from 1858 and 1860, but that proves nothing. 'Though the poem was probably in almost final form by 1861, it was probably retouched in 1863 when Hume was much in Browning's mind.' These probablys and a presumably leave us where we began. ' "Sludge" was probably the long poem, "which I have not seen a line of", recorded by Mrs. Browning on May 18, 1860'.

I propose a different probably, in the other direction. To one of the editors of the great Longman edition of Robert Browning's poetry, John Woolforde, I am obliged for information that in the manuscripts of *Dramatis Personae*, where 'Sludge' appeared in 1864, that poem has more corrections and afterthoughts than any others in the whole volume. Woolforde suggests that may be evidence of later composition, a fresh manuscript rather than fair and final copy. From another angle (not evidence, but my offering of a probably) one could imagine the Browning marriage which was singularly harmonious. Throwing out the wretched wreath was a surprising gesture, bad-tempered, shocking, but to have written that long poem without a word to her, a sustained release of aggression while this perfect union endured, would indeed suggest a different spleen, out of tune with their recorded lives.

It seems far simpler to suppose that he wrote 'Mr. Sludge' a couple of years after her death, looking back in anger upon the nuisance caused by Hume and his sycophants to all the shared honesty and art of their lives. A notion that he produced this furious poem, aimed as it would then have seemed at her folly no less than his deceptions, loving her in a state of suppressed opposition strikes me as grotesque.

---

[5]   CLXIX, 1957.
[6]   New York, 1955, p. 307.

The time has come to consider 'Mr. Sludge the Medium', and Browning's perceptions in that poem, about which Isabel Armstrong wrote the best analytical essay[7]. When he has put the issue of truth outside the terms of reason, we read there,

> and suggested that the intellect cannot be a means to knowledge, he can safely make an appeal to uncertainty. It cannot be ascertained that he is authentic, but equally, it cannot be ascertained that he is not ... Sludge's position is impregnable.

The larger point is that Browning, so thoroughly opposed, could imagine and understand, become Sludge's interpreter. Perhaps it had all begun half-innocently:

> Strictly, it's what good people style untruth;
> But yet, so far, not quite the full-grown thing:
> It's fancying, fable-making, nonsense-work –
> What never meant to be so very bad ...

I break off to recall the summer of 1934, when I was eleven years old and on holiday with my family in Cornwall. My parents had rented a pleasant white house above the sea, not far from Lizard Point, for the month of August. When some trouble threatened its water supply, the owner came over to advise us. I remember the elderly man in a brown suit, his white beard. He said, after explaining about the water, that he was a diviner, a dowser. This intrigued my father, a scientist *manqué*. A natural sceptic, he watched as the visitor cut his forked twig from a tamarisk tree and walked, as we all followed sensing the excitement. His twig turned up and over, moved by no visible force.

My father tried, without result; my mother, brother, sister. To be middle among five children, with no particular distinction, offered a temptation which I took upon impulse, claiming the stick in my hands forced itself over. Instant disbelief, of course, causing emphatic denial. Try again: I did. As accusations became a question mark it appeared I was on to a good thing. Confirming a lie at the age of eleven was not a troublesome matter; I bathed in the experience of being thus singled out. 'It's nothing clever you do', said my parents, anxious to guard me from conceit, 'just a gift'. But I liked gifts, and lacked them; just what the therapist ordered.

My water-divining lie showed signs of making good progress. Our bearded visitor offered an atmosphere of better courtesy than would

---

[7] Browning's *Mr. Sludge, "The Medium"*, *Victorian Poetry*, Vol. II, Winter 1964.

otherwise have greeted my claim. After he had gone I made the stick turn at other parts of the house and garden. Once my sister Rosalind, who later shared the discovery of the structure of DNA, saw me alone as I exercised the stick over one such place without turning it. 'I thought that's where you said there's supposed to be water'. 'Oh' I answered, caught out, 'I wasn't holding it properly'. She, none other, had observed me properly, and doubted.

And Mr. Sludge? Those lines from the long poem are so apt, they may as well be repeated:

> Strictly, it's what good people style untruth;
> But yet, so far, not quite the full-grown thing:
> It's fancying, fable-making, nonsense-work –
> What never meant to be so very bad ...

Sludge imagines the lad who says, knowing money to be a form of success, 'I've got a V-note'. (Nobody knows where, or whether Browning heard that term, a phoney Americanism for five-dollar bill). Anyway, the company suspects him of deceit or theft.

> 'Lies, Lies, Lies', you'd shout: and why?

But if the same boy, learning what fascination commonly followed any manifestation of ghosts or spirits, claimed such an experience for himself, the world would encourage his nonsense to the limits of patience.

> 'Tell it out!
> Don't fear us! Take your time, and recollect!
> Sit down first: try a glass of wine, my boy!'

And I, past the front lines of defence, recall just such a readiness to watch, attend, experiment. Once the conviction of a phenomenon took root, horizons extended. Explanations were sought, for whatever seemed for a puzzling moment less than convincing. Just so with the youthful Sludge:

> 'No haste!
> Pause and collect yourself! We understand!
> That's the bad memory, or the natural shock,
> Or the unexplained *phenomena*!'

And the inner circle became converted. Eleven years old, I never thought about the growing danger of a life discovered. Like Sludge at first,

> 'Tis but a foot in the water and out again.

We waded deeper, he and I. My father paid a few guineas for me to become a life member of the British Society of Dowsers. When they held their summer meeting at a huge house and estate, as it seemed then, Kirtlington Park near Oxford, the owner – whose name, H. M. Budgett is easily recalled – sent his secretary to accompany me from Paddington station; his large car met us at Oxford. Arranged in lines on his croquet lawn were upturned flower-pots, beneath several of which were placed a variety of metal bars, gold, silver, copper, iron perhaps. I had heard that by fixing a sample at the fork of my stick, it would respond in sympathy. By some odd chance one of my guesses was correct, the only – and thoroughly useless – lottery I ever won. I remember the loud-speaker announcement: ' ... and we report a success from the newest and youngest member of our fraternity'. One of the oldest predicted that I would become 'a really great scientist'; perhaps his dowsing was less faulty. *The Times* correspondent mentioned in his report 'one lad of eleven, who carried a forked hazel stick which anyone else of his age might have used for a catapult'. Was it largely, that summer meeting, a day of pretence? Few other finds among the flower-pots were shouted from loudspeakers. As to swivelling pendulums, dangling weights or my hazel sticks – as Sludge remarked:

> Who knows if you drive them or they drive you?

In a remarkable growth of Browning's perception of him, Sludge extended into ever deeper rubbish to hold his world's attention. It was their fault, he pleads, not his:

> I'll prove, you push on David till he dives
> And ends the shivering.

Table-rapping, nothing. Spirit-hands, inadequate. The accordion, held with one hand, not very convincing. His new trump card was auto-levitation which, in the vaguest of parallels which linked this imposture with religion, must have carried overtones of resurrection from the dead. At a séance in St. Petersburg, for example, after his second experiment in dynastic marriage:

> Mr. Hume presently declared that he felt himself being raised. He took, as he was lifted, a horizontal position, with his arms crossed on his breast; and in this reclining attitude was transported by invisible means into the middle of the apartment. After four or five minutes he was carried back in the same fashion to his old place at the table.[8]

---

8   Wyndham, *Mr. Sludge the Medium*, p. 238.

Two differing accounts of one event show what problems faced any ambitious medium. This is the account of a journalist, Trollope's friend Robert Bell:

> His voice was heard above our heads. He had risen from his chair to a height of four or five feet ... We watched in profound stillness, and saw his figure pass from one side of the window to the other. He hovered round the circle for several minutes and passed, this time perpendicularly, over our heads. I heard his voice behind me in the air. He now passed to the farthest extremity of the room, and we could judge by his voice of the attitude and distance he had attained. He had reached the ceiling, upon which he made a slight mark; and soon afterwards he descended and resumed his place at the table.[9]

A different interpretation appears in the report of a fictitious character called Christopher Kirkland, from a novel by Mrs. Lynn Linton:

> There was nothing to have prevented Mr. Hume from drawing the *chaise-longue* to himself by means of a string round the two frong legs; moving it by his own feet and muscles; standing on the centre of the ottoman; and, with a knife, fastened to the end of a stick, scratching a cross on the ceiling. The rest was easy to ventriloquism, and certain to credulity ... But no one was allowed to investigate, and, as to express doubt would have been impolite, things were received with acclaim by most of those present; and only a few of us had the honesty of silence.[10]

Browning shows how such as Kirkland were dismissed, out on their ears. Most among the assembly agree, accept, wonder –

> Here's your circle now:
> Two-thirds of them, with heads like you their host,
> Turn up their eyes, and cry, as you expect,
> 'Lord, who'd have thought it!' But there's always one
>
> Looks wise, compassionately smiles, submits
> 'Of your veracity no kind of doubt,
> But – do you feel so certain of that boy's'.

Appalling breach of manners! If that were so, all present would be proved fools. Wholly 'unacceptable', to use the current word. As Sludge says,

> Terrible were such catastrophe!
> So, evidence is redoubled, doubled again
> And doubled besides.

---

9   op. cit., p. 102.
10   op. cit., p. 103.

The disgracer is disgraced, forced to leave; the circle, more convinced than ever, closes ranks.

> So much for him,
> The black sheep, guest without the wedding-garb,
> The doubting Thomas!

I am amazed by Browning's truth. My father had slight acquaintance with a distinguished scientist, President of the Royal Institution, Sir William Bragg. It was there in Albermarle Street, I believe, that we went to tea. I remember his Edwardian face, white moustache, courteous manner. I was to be tested. By then, like Sludge, I had advanced into wilder ventures than turning the stick above water. Human bodies it responded to, dead or alive. Bragg placed himself in several parts of his drawing room, while I wandered across the room above with my stick, recording his position. Each time we 'found' him, my father stamped twice as a signal for him to shift from one spot to the next.

Analysing it, when he joined us again, Bragg was not impressed. It was his view that I had got it wrong. Of greater interest to me even then, aware that only by a miracle could it have been otherwise, was how my scientific father found reasons to believe that I had got it right. Bragg had moved at his first signal, he said, instead of taking that as the moment for beginning the test. But for the unlucky misunderstanding, he became convinced, my places of detection would have been accurate. As Sludge explains, with perfect conciseness,

> In short, a hit proves much, a miss proves more.

Sludge develops the theme, finds himself impregnable:

> I'll go yet a step further, and maintain,
> Once the imposture plunged its proper depth
> I' the rotten of your natures, all of you, –
> (If one's not mad nor drunk, and hardly then)
> It's impossible to cheat – that's, be found out!

Spoilsports, like John Stuart Mill, could be ignored. Accepting none of it, never ready to receive, he wrote in a letter to a friend:

> For my own part, I not only have never seen any evidence that I think of the slightest weight in favour of spiritualism, but I should also find it very difficult to believe any of it on any evidence whatever.

No damage there, from people who refused the possibility of witnessing evidence.

As to Hume, the achievements passed all guessing. Among his

believers was the Master of Lindsay, at whose house in Buckingham Gate a séance took place in December 1868. Lord Adare wrote an account of it:

> Lindsay suddenly said, 'Oh, good heavens! I know what he is going to do. It is too fearful! Adah says I must tell you. He is going out of the window, in the other room, and coming in at this window'.

That is what happened, and obviously something better is implied than a stroll round the balcony. Adare, asking how it could have happened, observed a test. 'The window, apparently, instead of being wide open, was not raised more than a few inches'. Hume then

> went through the open space, head first, quite rapidly, his body being horizontal and nearly rigid. He came in again, feet foremost, and we returned to the other room.

I also travelled one stage further – without really plotting it, but as the coach took me – upon a memorable afternoon with the then Dean of Westminster, Dr Foxley Norris, to whom my absurdities had been mentioned. He asked us to tea. The Dean sat relaxed with his legs spread wide, talking with me at a small table we shared. He took, it was said, a special interest in dowsing. With the particular skill – gift – alleged to be mine, after tea some of us walked the cloisters to detect (not difficult, I suppose) burial-places of dead abbots and his predecessors. The Dean did not accompany us upon this less than holy quest, and was too polite to deny us the pleasure of it. As Sludge said, it was easy to learn the knack:

> I'll play you twenty tricks miraculous
> To people untaught the trade ...
> I found it slip, easy as an old shoe.

Was there an element of truth in the lies of Sludge, or Hume, or in mine? Browning offered his answers clearly, subtly, as one would expect, for Sludge, a liar nine-tenths of the way beyond question:

> There's a real love of a lie,
> Liars find ready-made for lies they make,
> As hand for glove, or tongue for sugar-plum.

Yet he remains equivocal, too just a dramatist to view the man he loathes as total evil. Sludge is his Shylock, of whom till the final trumpet-sound of footnote squabble critics will argue. Sludge, like Shylock, was one who breathed and bled. Something weighed in the opposite balance, against his 'real love of a lie':

> I've my taste of truth,
> Likewise my touch of falsehood, – vice no doubt,
> But you've your vices also: I'm content.

And if the lies seemed at the brink of exposure, marvellous fantasy pushed back that horizon:

> Here's true life indeed,
> And the world well won now, mine for the first time.

I could tell something of that sort, in its infancy, too. One trick was to detect, blindfold, a coin held suddenly under the fork of my stick. Usually – try it – you are not without vision when a handkerchief is tied round your head. If by bad luck you are (as one wretched day when my headmaster said 'Now we'll make jolly sure you can't see' and used a scarf), reasonably acute perception will declare the moment when something is expected to happen. My father had read in the dowsing journal that if several people linked hands with the dowser and each other, so that he held the twig's left fork and someone else its right fork, everything would work as if he alone had control. We tried and, hazardously, over it went. This was done often, to my sense of guessing. They never puzzled me by extending that experiment from, say, five people to fifty. Had they tried, I might have pushed my luck too far. As things existed, undistinguished in the middle of our family of five, this was true life indeed and the world mine for the first time.

As I and my lie grew, alarm bells rang. I refused to perform for guests in the evening, or groups at school. My father, who in many things knew me quite well, blundered by interpreting this as the birth of modesty, a becoming reticence. And so it continued, the subject buried rather than forgotten, far too long. On leave from the navy, 1946, convalescent after tuberculosis, as we drove through Wales my father shocked me by stopping the car. 'We've had enough of this', he said, 'here's some hazel, I'm going to cut a twig for you to demonstrate'.

'I can't'.
'Why not?'
'I can't, never could'. Appalling silence.
'It was always a lie, I could never do it'. Deep breath. Life and the car proceeded again, in slow motion.
'If you've lost your power, that's one thing. I won't have you saying you could never do it'.

Was it a moment of truth – Sludge might have asked – or the moment of a lie?

Hume never created such bourgeois embarrassment, contrived to keep his show on the road; marrying rich Russians, performing, writing. 'Home was not a professional medium', Rigg's *DNB* note ends, 'and scupulously abstained from taking money for his séances'. To have left that impression, a sort of genius was needed. His profession gained him wide notoriety, social triumph, rich marriages and a scandalous fortune. It was Elizabeth Browning's opinion that 'We ... when we enter the spirit-land, see our friends under the appearance which they had on earth, otherwise we could not recognise them'. Long before ever Hume entered the spirit-land, Robert was able to view him with amazing clarity.[11]

'Mr. Sludge the Medium' has not held a place among the best known or most admired of his poems. A critic in *The St. James's Magazine*, July 1864 – none other than Robert Bell who had watched and reported Hume's amazing levitation – singled out its particular merit as a fault: 'It is very like Mr. Browning to make his medium feel deeply conscious of the pathos which is woven in with the hypocrisy of his profession. But it is *not* like Sludge'. The *British Quarterly Review* in 1880 had a simpler position: 'We vastly prefer *May and Death*, and some of the simpler lyrics'. This essay offers no conclusion, or point of view, beyond admiration for Browning's intellectual analysis of the man who had seemed for many years to damage him; and a conviction that Sludge was written after Elizabeth's death.

[11] I have not cast into the balance a defence of Hume by the poet Elizabeth Jennings, *The Shadow and the Light*, 1982, which relies upon Hume's books and those of his widow.